Alpine Cupcakes, Inc.

Audit Case Study

Part II

Alpine Cupcakes, Inc.
Balance Sheets as of 3/31/20X2 and 12/31/20X1 (USD $)
Audit Year December 31, 20X2

PBC

B.3.1

Balance Sheet:	As of 3/31/20X2	As of 12/31/20X1	As of 3/31/20X1
Current Assets			
Cash: Storefront	$125,498.76	$135,135.15	$142,293.51
Cash: Corporate Accounts	296,685.79	212,976.82	67,673.10
Cash: Payroll	123,432.43	124,726.15	122,931.81
Accounts Receivable	120,324.46	191,451.64	158,766.71
Office Supplies	2,379.00	2,604.00	2,133.00
Cooking Supplies	4,777.00	4,713.00	3,808.00
Inventory: Ingredients	25,190.66	25,580.09	26,779.44
Inventory: Cake Boxes and Cupcake Cups	1,423.05	1,190.10	434.95
Inventory: Beverages	3,340.30	3,260.80	2,348.50
Total Current Assets	**$703,051.45**	**$701,637.75**	**$527,169.02**
Long-term Assets			
Equipment	150,180.00	150,180.00	150,180.00
Accumulated Depreciation: Equipment	82,455.00	(78,828.00)	(66,372.00)
Plant & Property	330,000.00	330,000.00	330,000.00
Accumulated Depreciation: Plant & Property	82,500.00	(79,200.00)	(69,300.00)
Land	125,000.00	125,000.00	125,000.00
Total Long-term assets	**$440,225.00**	**$447,152.00**	**$469,508.00**
Total Assets	**$1,143,276.45**	**$1,148,789.75**	**$996,677.02**
Liabilities			
Accounts Payable	25,712.00	38,556.70	40,168.65
Wage Taxes Payable	0.00	0.00	0.00
Income Tax Payable	21,247.78	38,125.96	18,683.65
Dividends Payable	0.00	13,125.00	0.00
Mortgage Payable	290,673.81	292,262.13	296,909.93
Notes Payable: Vehicles	22,555.53	24,878.31	31,659.28
Total Liabilities	**$360,189.12**	**$406,948.10**	**$387,421.51**
Stockholders' Equity			
Common Stock	50,000.00	50,000.00	50,000.00
Additional Paid in Capital	120,921.00	120,921.00	120,921.00
Retained Earnings	612,166.33	570,920.65	438,334.50
Total Stockholders' Equity	**$783,087.33**	**$741,841.65** B.2.1	**$609,255.50**
Total Liabilities and Stockholders' Equity	**$1,143,276.45**	**$1,148,789.75**	**$996,677.02**

Alpine Cupcakes, Inc.
Income Statements for the 3 Months Ended 3/31/20X2 and 3/31/20X1 (USD $)
Audit Year December 31, 20X2

PBC

B.3.2

	03/31/20X2	03/31/20X1
Revenue		
Sales Revenue: Corporate Accounts	$353,739.58	$365,450.08
Sales Revenues: Storefront	80,649.00	60,000.00
Total Sales Revenue	**$434,388.58**	**$425,450.08**
Cost of Goods Sold: Ingredients	66,736.39	59,623.00
Cost of Goods Sold: Boxes and Cupcake Cups	3,875.55	3,755.55
Cost of Goods Sold: Beverages	5,466.50	5,681.50
Total COGS	**$76,078.44**	**$69,060.05**
Gross Profit	**$358,310.14**	**$356,390.03**
Interest Revenue	89.00	65.00
Gross Profit Plus Interest Revenue	**$358,399.14**	**$356,455.03**
Expenses		
Wage Expense	216,719.00	217,791.00
Wage Tax Expense	17,971.24	18,077.94
Medical Insurance Expense	8,100.00	8,100.00
Auto Insurance Expense	1,035.00	1,035.00
Interest Expense	3,996.90	4,197.69
Electrical & Gas Service Expense	1,523.20	1,708.00
Liability Insurance Expense	3,768.40	3,693.60
Telecommunications Expense	472.50	462.00
Cell Phone Service Expense	912.00	933.00
Postage Expense	139.50	135.90
Professional Services Expense	2,070.00	2,122.50
Maintenance Expense	1,212.00	1,132.00
Office Supplies Expense	8,050.00	7,342.00
Dry Cleaning Expense	398.75	416.15
Storefront Paper Supplies Expense	778.25	869.00
Rental Expense	4,752.00	4,752.00
Waste Services Expense	150.00	150.00
Car Maintenance and Fuel Expense	995.38	1,026.78
Repair Expense	372.50	381.25
Water Expense	378.75	373.75
Soda Machine Repair and CO2 Expense	1,156.00	1,128.00
Credit Card Expense	878.31	897.89
Cooking Supplies Expense	12,704.00	16,880.64
Banking Fees	445.00	445.00
Selling and Administrative Expenses	**$288,978.68**	**$294,051.09**
Depreciation Expense: Equipment	3,627.00	4,152.00
Depreciation Expense: Plant & Property	3,300.00	3,300.00
Total Depreciation Expense	**$6,927.00**	**$7,452.00**
Total Expenses	**$295,905.68**	**$301,503.09**

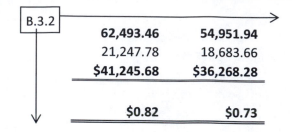

Alpine Cupcakes, Inc.
Income Statements for the 3 Months Ended 3/31/20X2 and 3/31/20X1 (USD $)
Audit Year December 31, 20X2

PBC

	B.3.2		
Earnings Before Income Taxes		62,493.46	54,951.94
Income Tax Expense		21,247.78	18,683.66
Net Income		**$41,245.68**	**$36,268.28**
Earnings per Share		**$0.82**	**$0.73**

Garcia and Foster, CPAs

Performed by: SDM	**Reviewed by:** *TKJ*
Date: 9/15/20X2	**Date:** *2/14/20X3*

Materiality Methodology:
Planning materiality (PM) is determined as follows:
(2) For public clients, we base materiality on 4% of prior year's net income unless the client is at a loss or close to break even, in which case we base materiality on 1% of total assets.
(3) For private clients, we base materiality on 1% of prior year's equity.

Tolerable misstatement (TM) is set at 50% of PM.
Summary of audit differences (SAD) threshold is set at 5% of PM.
We will place any identified misstatements greater than our SAD threshold onto the SAD listing.
During our evaluations of overall misstatements, we will compare the total of misstatements on the SAD listing to our PM threshold.

Application of Methodology to Alpine Audit for 20X2:

20X1 Total Equity for Alpine Cupcakes, Inc.: \$741,842 (B.1.1)
Materiality thresholds for the 20X2 audit:

$PM = 0.01 \times \$741,842 = \$7,418 \approx \$7,400$
$TM = 0.50 \times \$7,400 = \$3,700$
$SAD = 0.05 \times \$7,400 = \$370$

Determine Inherent Risk, Control Risk, and Detection Risk:
During the planning of the audit, including understanding the client and its environment and understanding the internal control environment, we must determine the level of inherent risk (IR), control risk (CR) and detection risk (DR).

Application of IR, CR, and DR for 20X2 Alpine Audit:
Our preliminary risk assessment levels are set as follows:

Audit Risk	=	Low
Inherent risk	=	High
Control risk	=	Moderate
Detection risk	=	High

We have set our risk assessment levels for the overall audit in order to reduce our audit risk to the appropriate level.

Alpine Cupcakes, Inc.
Audit Risk Assessment Memo
Audit Year December 31, 20X2

Performed by: SDM
Date: 9/15/20x2

Reviewed by: *TKJ*
Date: *2/14/20X3*

Fraud Brainstorming:
To comply with PCAOB ASC 2110, *Identifying and Assessing Risks of Material Misstatements*, the firm requires all engagement team personnel to be involved in a brainstorming session, during which team members exchange ideas about how and where the client's financial statements may be susceptible to material misstatement due to fraud.

Documentation:

As required, Tryg Johnson and I conducted a fraud brainstorming session on February 6, 20X3. Overall we find the client to be highly ethical. Owner Alexis Madison has the highest integrity and has strong ties to the community. Tryg and I concluded that there was little or no risk of material misstatement due to fraud at Alpine and no accounts for which fraud was a concern.

Simon Malik   *Tryg Johnson*

Understanding of Client's Environment Including Internal Controls:

We reviewed the client's background information retained in our PERM FILE workpapers to understand the company and its inherent risk. We will also perform an understanding of internal controls over the client's processes prior to our test of control procedures (see audit program.) Through performing preliminary analytical procedures, we also assessed any significant changes within the company's accounts and activities (see WPs B.3.1 through B.3.3.) Per discussion with Alexis Madison, there are no significant changes within the company beyond the consideration of issuing debt.
SDM

Account Balances and Transaction Risk Assessment:

Per our review of the account balances and transactions, we have assessed a higher level for the risk of material misstatement in the following accounts:
Inventory (due to inventory price fluctuations)
Revenue (potential fictitious sales could lead to overstated revenues)
Accounts Receivable (potential fictitious sales transactions could lead to AR overstatement)
We believe that there is a higher likelihood for material misstatements in these accounts.

SDM

Overall Risk Assessment Summary:

Based on our preliminary analytical procedures, and knowledge of the client, we assess inherent risk as high and control risk as medium, making detection risk high.
Simon Malik

Performed by:
SDM 10/1/20X2
Reviewed by:
TKJ 10/9/20X2

B.1.1

Further

	As of 3/31/20X2	As of 12/31/20X1	$ Change	% Change	
Current Assets					
Cash: Storefront	$125,498.76	$135,135.15	($8,636.39)	-6.39%	1
Cash: Corporate Accounts	296,685.79	212,976.82	84,708.97	39.77%	1
Cash: Payroll	123,432.43	124,726.15	(293.72)	-0.24%	✓
Accounts Receivable	120,324.46	191,451.64	(70,127.18)	-36.63%	2
Office Supplies	2,379.00	2,604.00	775.00	29.76%	✓
Cooking Supplies	4,777.00	4,713.00	1,064.00	22.58%	✓
Inventory: Ingredients	25,190.66	25,580.09	610.57	2.39%	✓
Inventory: Cake Boxes and Cupcake Cups	1,423.05	1,190.10	1,232.95	103.60%	✓
Inventory: Beverages	3,340.30	3,260.80	1,079.50	33.11%	✓
Total Current Assets	**$703,051.45**	**$701,637.75**			
Long-Term Assets					
Equipment	150,180.00	150,180.00	0.00	0.00%	✓
A/D: Equipment	(82,455.00)	(78,828.00)	3,627.00	4.60%	✓
Plant & Property	330,000.00	330,000.00	0.00	0.00%	✓
A/D: Plant & Property	(82,500.00)	(79,200.00)	3,300.00	-4.17%	✓
Land	125,000.00	125,000.00	0.00	0.00%	✓
Total Long-Term assets	**440,225.00**	**$447,152.00**			
Total Assets	**$1,143,276.45**	**$1,148,789.75**			
Liabilities					
Accounts Payable	$25,712.00	38,556.70	(12,844.70)	-33.31%	3
Wage Taxes Payable	0.00	0.00	0.00	0.00%	✓
Income Tax Payable	21,247.78	38,125.96	(16,878.18)	-44.27%	4
Dividends Payable	0.00	13,125.00	(13,125.00)	-100.00%	5
Mortgage Payable	290,673.81	292,262.13	(1,588.32)	-0.54%	✓
Notes Payable: Vehicles	22,555.53	24,878.31	(2,322.78)	-9.34%	✓
Total Liabilities	**360,189.12**	**$406,948.10**			
Stockholders' Equity					
Common Stock, par value $1.00; Authorized 1,000,000; Issued and outstanding 50,000	50,000.00	50,000.00	0.00	0.00%	✓
Additional Paid in Capital	120,921.00	120,921.00	0.00	0.00%	✓
Retained Earnings	612,166.33	570,920.65	41,245.68	7.22%	✓
Total Stockholders' Equity	**783,087.33**	**$741,841.65**			
Total Liabilities and Stockholders' Equity	**$1,143,276.45**	**$1,148,789.75**			

F

✓ - The fluctuation is less than TM ($13,700) and less than a 10% change.
F – Footed

Alpine Cupcakes, Inc.
Preliminary Analytical Procedures—Balance Sheets
Audit Year December 31, 20X2

1 - We discussed the fluctuation in the cash accounts with Miguel Lopez, Store Manager and Cash Receipts Accounting. He stated that cash fluctuates drastically depending on the timing of cash receipts and disbursements. The company tries to keep less cash in the storefront account and more cash in the operating account to earn more interest. The company has not had a significant purchase in the past year, so the overall cash balance has significantly increased. The company plans to purchase some new cooking equipment in the next year to expand the business and take on some new accounts. In addition, the company has paid down some debt.

2 - We discussed the lower AR balance from prior year with Lisa Mercer, Corporate Sales Representative. She noted that the company has seen a slight decline in Corporate Sales primarily due to having two customers reducing their purchases in 20x2. These two customers are Luigi's Bistro and Mountain Lion Restaurant. In addition, the Company has made new efforts to collect from its customers in a timelier manner. If a customer does not pay in 30 days, Alpine calls the customer weekly to discuss and requests payment as soon as possible.

3 - We discussed changes in Accounts Payable with Lindsay McKenna. She noted that the company experienced a slight dip in purchase prices and the amount of purchases in Q1 20x2 in all of the vendors' accounts except for Mountain Dairy Company. The company expects sales to increase in Q2, so that payables will be in line with previous year activity with vendors. Milk prices have been increasing, so there is a concern that the cost of production will go up with milk and potentially sugar costs throughout 20x2. In addition, Lindsay stated that this change in the account is immaterial to the company's financial statements and is a reasonable fluctuation in this type of business.

4 – Per discussion with Miguel Lopez, the company paid the income tax payable amount of $38,125.96 from Q4 in 20x1 on January 15, 20x2. The new balance of $21,247.78 relates to the first quarter 20x2 income tax expense. The company pays its income taxes on a quarterly basis.

5 – Miguel stated that the dividends payable was paid in the first quarter 20x2 on April 24, 20x2 to Wasatch Range Trust. The company pays the dividends on an annual basis.

Alpine Cupcakes, Inc.
Preliminary Analytical Procedures—Quarterly Income Statements
Audit Year December 31, 20X2

B.1.2

	3 Months 03/31/20X2	3 Months 03/31/20X1	$ Change	% Change	
Statement of Profit and Loss					
Sales Revenue: Corporate Accounts	$353,739.58	$365,450.08	(11,710.50)	-3.20%	1
Sales Revenues: Storefront	80,649.00	60,000.00	20,649.00	34.42%	1
Total Sales Revenue	**434,388.58**	**425,450.08**	8,938.50	2.20%	1
Cost of Goods Sold: Ingredients	66,736.39	59,623.00	7,113.39	11.93%	1
Cost of Goods Sold: Boxes and Cupcake Cups	3,875.55	3,755.55	120.00	3.20%	1
Cost of Goods Sold: Beverages	5,466.50	5,681.50	(215.00)	-3.78%	1
Total COGS	**76,078.44**	**69,060.05**	7,018.39	10.16%	1
Gross Profit	**358,310.14**	**356,390.03**			
Interest Revenue	89.00	65.00	24.00	36.92%	✓
Gross Profit Plus Interest Revenue	**358,399.14**	**356,455.03**			
Expenses					
Wage Expense	216,719.00	217,791.00	(1,072.00)	−0.49%	✓
Tax Expense	17,971.24	18,077.94	(106.70)	−0.59%	✓
Medical Insurance Expense	8,100.00	8,100.00	0.00	0.00%	✓
Auto Insurance Expense	1,035.00	1,035.00	0.00	0.00%	✓
Interest Expense	3,996.90	4,197.69	(200.79)	−4.78%	✓
Electrical & Gas Service Expense	1,523.20	1,708.00	(184.80)	−10.82%	✓
Liability Insurance Expense	3,768.40	3,693.60	74.80	2.03%	✓
Telecommunications Expense	472.50	462.00	10.50	2.27%	✓
Cell Phone Service Expense	912.00	933.00	(21.00)	−2.25%	✓
Postage Expense	139.50	135.90	3.60	2.65%	✓
Professional Services Expense	2,070.00	2,122.50	(52.50)	−2.47%	✓
Maintenance Expense	1,212.00	1,132.00	80.00	7.07%	✓
Office Supplies Expense	8,050.00	7,342.00	708.00	9.64%	✓
Dry Cleaning Expense	398.75	416.15	(17.40)	−4.18%	✓
Storefront Paper Supplies Expense	778.25	869.00	(90.75)	−10.44%	✓
Rental Expense	4,752.00	4,752.00	0.00	0.00%	✓
Waste Services Expense	150.00	150.00	0.00	0.00%	✓

Alpine Cupcakes, Inc.
Preliminary Analytical Procedures—Quarterly Income Statements
Audit Year December 31, 20X2

B.1.2

	3 Months Ended 03/31/20X2	3 Months Ended 03/31/20X1	$ Change	% Change	
Expenses (continued)					
Car Maintenance and Fuel Expense	995.38	1,026.78	(31.40)	−3.06%	✓
Repair Expense	372.50	381.25	(8.75)	−2.30%	✓
Water Expense	378.75	373.75	5.00	1.34%	✓
Soda Machine Repair and CO2 Expense	1,156.00	1,128.00	28.00	2.48%	✓
Credit Card Expense	878.31	897.89	(19.58)	−2.18%	✓
Cooking Supplies Expense	12,704.00	16,880.64	(4,176.64)	−24.74%	2
Banking Fees	445.00	445.00	0.00	0.00%	✓
Selling and Administrative Expenses	**288,978.68**	**294,051.09**			
Depreciation Expense: Equipment	3,627.00	4,152.00	(525.00)	−12.64%	✓
Depreciation Expense: Plant & Property	3,300.00	3,300.00	0.00	0.00%	✓
Total Depreciation Expense	**6,927.00**	**7,452.00**			
Total Expenses	**295,905.68**	**301,503.09**			
Earnings Before Income tax	**138,482.90**	**123,946.99**			
Income Tax Expense	21,247.78	18,683.66	2,564.12	13.72%	✓
Net Income	**$117,235.12**	**$105,263.33**			
	F				

Auditor Notes:

✓ - The fluctuation is less than TM ($13,700) and less than a 10% change.

F – Footed

1 - The Company has experienced an overall increase in total sales of about 2% while COGS overall has increased by 10%. The Company has seen an increase in storefront sales through a recent increase in its Facebook following and more people learning about the Company's reputation for quality. The Company is seeing more birthday party orders where local customers are picking up their goods on the day of the event. The slight decline in corporate accounts revenue is primarily due to two customers: Luigi's Bistro and Mountain Lion Restaurant. The Company expects corporate sales to pick up through the rest of the year. The increase in costs of goods sold is due to both the overall increase in sales and to recent increases in milk and sugar prices.

2 - We discussed the significant change in the cooking supplies expense account with Lindsay McKenna. Lindsay said the increase in cooking supplies expense is due to higher prices from one supplier, Rocky Mountain Kitchen Goods. The Company is working with Rocky Mountain to try to receive better prices on its cooking supplies purchases. Particularly, the Company notices that prices on cooking pans and cooking sheets used in baking the cupcakes increased by 20%.

Alpine Cupcakes, Inc.
Preliminary Analytical Procedures—Ratio Analysis
Audit Year December 31, 20X2

	Company Ratios		
	3/31/20X2	3/31/20X1	% Change
Current Ratio **	11.367	7.105	60%	1, μ
Quick Ratio**	10.882	6.707	62%	1, μ
Receivables Turnover	2.940	2.302	28%	2, μ
Days Outstanding in Receivables	124.155	158.571	-22%	2, μ
Inventory Turnover	2.540	2.336	9%	√, μ
Days of Inventory on Hand	143.710	156.247	-8%	√, μ
Gross Profit Percentage	4.710	5.161	-9%	√, μ
Profit Margin	0.095	0.085	11%	3, μ
Return on Assets	0.036	0.036	-1%	√, μ
Return on Equity	0.053	0.060	-12%	4, μ
Debt to Assets	0.274	0.330	-17%	5, μ
Debt to Equity	0.400	0.539	-26%	5, μ

	Industry Ratios					
	March 20X2			March 20X1		
	Avg	Min	Max	Avg	Min	Max
Current Ratio	5.55	1.05	15.30	5.70	2.02	13.76
Quick Ratio	4.50	0.77	14.00	4.54	1.06	12.45
Receivables Turnover	2.97	1.28	5.68	2.66	1.09	4.41
Days Outstanding in Receivables	150.08	64.30	285.43	159.54	82.83	333.76
Inventory Turnover	1.62	0.24	3.95	1.51	0.20	4.15
Days of Inventory on Hand	441.54	92.29	1525.44	458.39	87.88	1830.71
Gross Profit Percentage	0.31	0.01	0.49	0.33	0.10	0.48
Profit Margin	0.02	-0.09	0.10	0.11	-0.09	1.02
Return on Assets	0.01	-0.03	0.04	0.04	-0.02	0.29
Return on Equity	0.04	-0.04	0.23	0.08	-0.16	0.67
Debt to Assets	0.21	0.00	0.74	0.19	0.00	0.55
Debt to Equity	0.26	-0.05	1.76	0.58	0.00	3.99

Auditor Notes:

** Calculation includes current portion of Mortgage payable and Notes Payable based on client's
amortization schedule. On 3/31/20X2, the current portions of the mortgage and notes payables are
$6,555.19 and $8,337.88, respectively. On 3/31/20X1, the current portions of the mortgage and notes
payables are $6,236.12 and $9,103.75, respectively.

√ - Fluctuation meets expectations of being less than a 10% change. → greater than 10%

μ - The 20X2 ratio is within the expected range (between the min and max) of the industry data. → outside of min & max

Auditor Notes (continued)

Ratio Calculations

ST Liquidity Ratios: Ability to Meet ST Obligations

$Current\ Ratio = Current\ Assets \div Current\ Liabilities$

$Quick\ Ratio = (Current\ Assets - Inventories) \div Current\ Liabilities$

Activity Ratios: How Effectively Assets Are Managed

$Receivables\ Turnover = Credit\ Sales \div Receivables$

$Days\ Receivables\ Outstanding = 365 \div Receivables\ Turnover$

$Inventory\ Turnover = COGS \div Inventory$

$Days\ Inventory\ on\ Hand = 365 \div Inventory\ Turnover$

Profitability Ratios

$Gross\ Profit\ Percentage = (Sales - COGS) \div Sales$

$Profit\ Margin = Net\ Income \div Net\ Sales$

$Return\ on\ Assets = Net\ Income \div Total\ Assets$

$Return\ on\ Equity = Net\ Income \div Total\ Stockholder's\ Equity$

Coverage Ratio: Long-Term Solvency (Ability of Entity to Continue as a Going Concern)

$Debt\ to\ Equity = (ST\ Debt + LT\ Debt) \div Stockholders'\ Equity$

1- Current assets significantly increased primarily due to an increase in corporate cash account of $335,884.72. As noted in our balance sheet analysis (B.2.1), Miguel Lopez says cash fluctuates drastically depending on the timing of cash receipts and purchases. The company has not made any major purchases in the past year, but plans to make some purchases in 20x3. In addition, the current liabilities in 20x2 have decreased from prior year primarily due to the timing of paying accounts payable balances and the timing of purchases.

2- The Company is collecting its receivables more quickly than it has in prior years. Per our discussion with Lisa Mercer, the Company is taking additional steps to have customers pay in a more timely manner by improving customer relationships and calling customers weekly when the customers have past due balances.

3 - The Company's profit margin has increased since prior year due to increases in storefront sales and decreases in the Company's selling and administrative expenses. Per discussion with Miguel Lopez, the Company has seen great growth and has performed well in relation to the industry competitors, largely because the Company has built its reputation for quality and has maintained good relationships with vendors to keep costs down.

4 – The company's ROE is significantly lower than prior year. We have requested a time to meet with Miguel Lopez to discuss the difference in this ratio in comparison to our expectations.

5 - The company's debt to assets and debt to equity ratios have decreased from prior year due to the decrease in the long-term liabilities, along with the decreases in current accounts payable (due to timing of purchases and payments of liabilities).

Alpine Cupcakes, Inc.
Cash Narrative
Audit Year December 31, 20X2

Garcia and Foster, CPAs

Performed by: *ARO*   **Reviewed by:** *TES*
Date: *1/15/20X3*   **Date:** *01/22/20X3*

The following narrative documents discussions with client personnel to obtain an understanding of their cash processes. Each year, we review and update the narrative with the client, as well as walk through the cash receipts and cash disbursements processes. To update the narrative for 20X2, I spoke with Miguel Lopez (store manager), Lindsay McKenna (cash receipt and bank reconciliation functions), Priscilla Orr (cash disbursements), and Diana Hayes (assistant store manager).

Cash Receipts Process

On average, about 80% of Alpine's revenues are from sales to business accounts—primarily restaurants, hotels, coffee shops, deli shops, and bulk food service distributors. Customers pay by check as Alpine does not have an online method to receive payments. The assistant store manager (Diana Hayes) sorts the mail each day. To maintain confidentiality of the contents, Diana does not open the mail, but delivers it unopened to the appropriate department. She sends mail received from customers to the store manager, Miguel Lopez. Every Friday, Miguel opens the envelopes containing customer payments and writes on the back of each check received an endorsement, "Alpine." [He explains that his hand would get too tired if he wrote out the entire name.] He throws away any remittance advices sent with the checks. Next, Miguel logs into the accounting system and posts the cash receipts to customers' accounts. He adds up the checks, writes the total amount on a bank deposit slip, paper-clips the checks together and places them on top of his desk as a reminder that he needs to go to the bank. The next business day (usually Monday), either Miguel or Lindsey McKenna (cash receipt clerk) takes the checks to the bank. Miguel explains that he typically withholds $100 cash from the deposit to use for minor office expenses such as coffee and donuts. After making the deposit, Miguel takes the receipt from the bank and places it in his "in-basket" so that if there are any problems with the bank he can easily find the appropriate deposit slip.

The remaining revenues (approximately 20%) are from storefront sales. Each cupcake sales associate works one day on storefront sales and the remaining time during the week on meeting the needs of his or her assigned business customers. In addition, each sales associate is encouraged to work on attaining new business accounts. Three sales associates work in the storefront on a daily basis. The sales associates answer customer questions and receive customer payments at the cash register. Diana Hayes (assistant store manager) also answers questions and helps out at the cash register. At the beginning of each day, Diana places the necessary cash in the register. Currently, the company keeps $300 from the prior day's sales as the next day's starting cash. The cash is kept in Diana's desk overnight. At the end of the day, one of the sales associates counts up the cash in the register and gives the cash register tape and cash to Diana Hayes. Diana reviews the cash and cash register tape and then gives the cash to Miguel Lopez. Miguel prepares a deposit slip for the week's receipts, and deposits the cash received from storefront sales along with customer receipts into the bank at the beginning of the next business day. Miguel reconciles the bank deposit receipts to the cash register tapes and the company deposit slips on a weekly basis.

Alpine Cupcakes, Inc.
Cash Narrative
Audit Year December 31, 20X2

Performed by: *ARO*
Date: *1/15/20X3*

Reviewed by: *TES*
Date: *01/22/20X3*

Cash Disbursements Process

The cash disbursements process begins at the origination of a request to purchase an item or service. Most purchase requisitions come from the cupcake specialists— Joshua Siedel, Lynn Carzoli, Samantha Hill, Brian Jensen, Carlos Menendez, and Julie Chen. Gabrielle Krause, Chef and Receiving Department Manager, reviews and approves purchases relating to operations and cupcake production. Miguel Lopez approves all administrative purchases. Once Gabrielle or Miguel signs the requisition indicating approval of the purchase, it is forwarded to Priscilla Orr, who places the order. She sends copies of the purchase order to Miguel and Gabrielle.

When goods are received, the receiving department counts the items and issues a receiving report, including the date received, vendor, and quantity. Copies of the receiving reports go to Gabrielle Krause, Miguel Lopez, and Priscilla Orr. Priscilla records receipt of the items in the inventory control records. Next, she prepares a voucher packet reconciling items, quantities, vendors, and prices from the approved purchase requisition and receiving report to the vendor's invoice. She then reconciles these amounts with those recorded in the general ledger to make sure inventory is recorded in the proper accounting period. Occasionally, Priscilla receives an invoice from an unfamiliar or new vendor who is not in the Alpine A/P system. In that case, she makes sure there is an associated receiving report and purchase requisition, and then adds the vendor information into the accounts payable system.

Weekly, Priscilla prepares checks to be signed by Miguel Lopez. The check log details include the check number, the payee, and the amount. Priscilla accounts for the check sequence each time she writes a new check, making sure the next check is the right number. She shreds any voided checks so that they cannot be misappropriated and reused. Priscilla keeps blank checks on a shelf in her office so that they are available to others if she is out of the office. Miguel reviews the voucher packet documentation and signs the check. Any checks over $5,000 must be co-signed by Alexis Madison. Once the check is signed, Miguel returns the checks to Priscilla for mailing. If Miguel is planning to be out of the office for an extended time, he signs 10 to 15 blank checks in advance and gives them to Priscilla so that the company's business can continue in his absence.

Alpine maintains a petty cash box to reimburse employees for small daily expenditures. Diana Hayes (assistant store manager) acts as custodian. To get reimbursed, the employee must have a receipt. Diana keeps the receipts in the box with the cash. At the end of the month, she makes journal entries for the expenses, counts the cash, and replenishes the cash box.

Bank Reconciliation Process

Lindsay McKenna reconciles the bank accounts monthly. Lindsay begins by inputting the ending cash balances per bank and general ledger into a reconciliation template. She reconciles last month's outstanding check registers, the outstanding checks listed on the last month's bank reconciliation, and this month's outstanding check register. This process verifies that all checks clearing the bank are removed from the outstanding check register and also identifies any new checks to be included if they have not

Performed by: *ARO*

Date: *1/15/20X3*

Reviewed by: *TES*

Date: *01/22/20X3*

Bank Reconciliation Process (continued)

cleared the bank. Lindsay lists the outstanding checks on the bank reconciliation, including the check number and amount. Any outstanding checks greater than 90 days are voided. Lindsay attempts to follow up with the vendor prior to voiding. If necessary (e.g., if the vendor did not receive the check), a new check is issued.

Any deposits made at the end of the month that have not cleared the bank per the bank statement are included as deposits in transit. Lindsay reviews all deposits for 5 days before month end to ensure they are handled properly in the reconciliation process.

Lindsay McKenna reviews the bank statement for any bank charges or other items that have not been recorded as of month end. Other common reconciling items include interest earned, NSF checks deposited, bank fees, Notes receivable and payable, and any corresponding interest. An adjusting journal entry is made for any transactions that need to be recorded for month end in relation to the balance per the book.

Miguel Lopez reviews and signs off on the reconciliations. Any unreconciled differences older than 3 months are written off as a miscellaneous expense after a full review and investigation by Lindsay.

Alpine Cupcakes, Inc.
Cash Flowcharts
Audit Year December 31, 20X2

Garcia and Foster, CPAs

Performed by: *ARO*   **Reviewed by:** *TES*
Date: *1/15/20X3*   **Date:** *01/22/20X3*

Cash Receipts—Corporate Accounts Receivable Flowchart

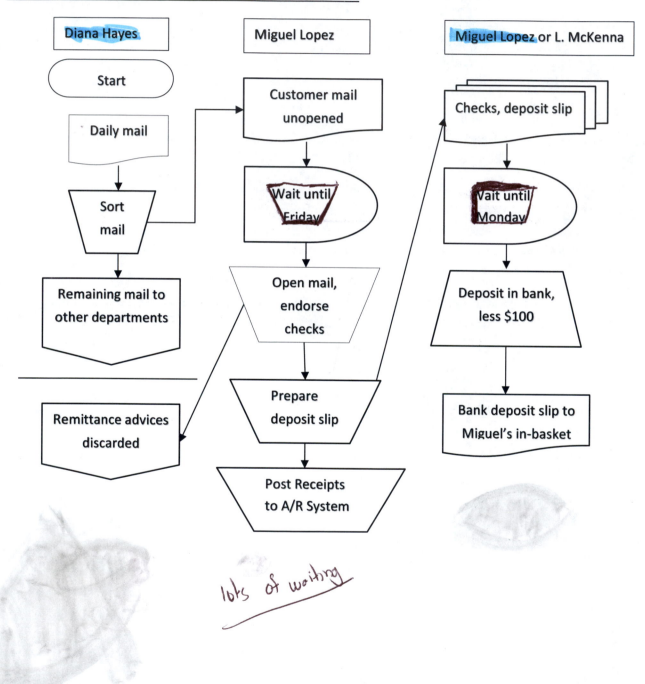

lots of waiting

Alpine Cupcakes, Inc.
Cash Flowcharts
Audit Year December 31, 20X2

Performed by: *ARO*   **Reviewed by:** *TES*

Date: *1/15/20X3*   **Date:** *01/22/20X3*

Cash Receipts—Storefront Flowchart

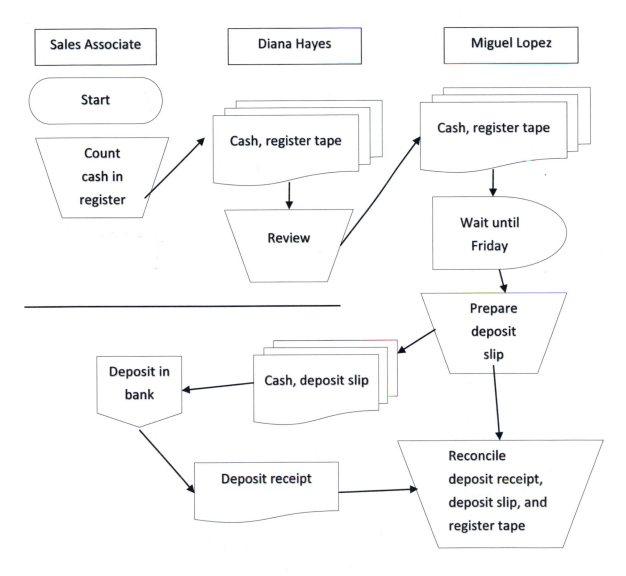

Performed by: *ARO*　　　　　　　　　　　　　　　　**Reviewed by:** *TES*
Date: *1/15/20X3*　　　　　　　　　　　　　　　　　**Date:** *01/22/20X3*

Cash Disbursements Flowchart

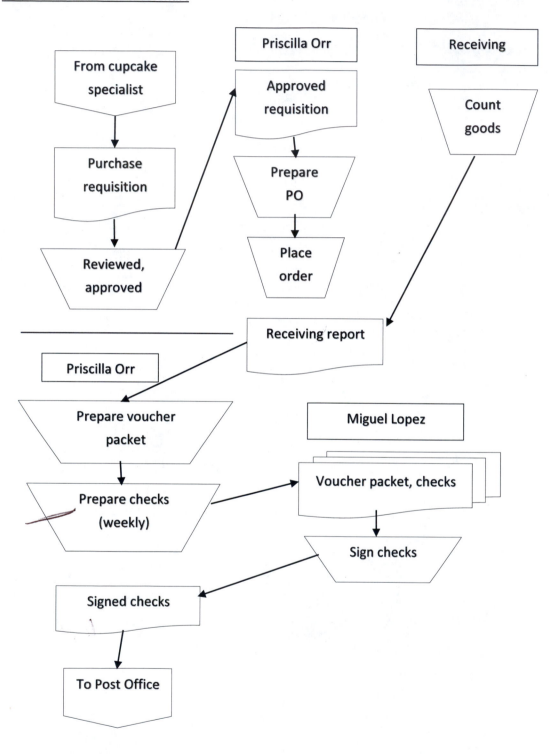

Alpine Cupcakes, Inc.
Cash Receipts, Disbursements, and Reconciliation TOC Memo
Audit Year December 31, 20X2

Garcia and Foster, CPAs

Performed By: *ARO*   **Reviewed By:** *TES*
Date: *2/4/20X3*   **Date:** *02/06/20X3*

Cash Receipts TOC:

I discussed with Diana Hayes the need to obtain the October and November mailroom control listings. Per Miguel's discussion, Diana Hayes was unable to perform the November mailroom control listing because she did not have enough time and she was out on vacation for one week. Therefore, Diana gave me the October and December control listing logs. To perform my testing of controls procedures, I conducted a surprise check on 2/07/20X3 to determine if Diana Hayes was inputting checks accurately and in a timely manner. During the surprise check, I found that Diana had been out sick for a few days, so she had all of the checks from 2/01/20X3 through the 7th. She was backdating the dates on the mailroom control listing to coincide with when they were received by the company. For any days that Diana missed in 20X2, she would perform the same tasks of backdating checks. The checks were kept on her desk until she had time to enter them into the mailroom control listing.

Per my review of the internal controls, I found that the cash receipt controls were operating effectively. The following controls were working properly:

- Lindsay McKenna reconciles the total on the monthly control listing to the cash receipts subledger and GL.
- Diana inputs the entries on a daily basis into the control listing.
- Miguel Lopez reviews and signs off on the monthly control listing by the 2nd day of the following month.

Cash Disbursements TOC:
I obtained the 6 largest cash disbursements that were made in December 20X2 from the December check log. The following Items were chosen to test controls related to the cash disbursements process:

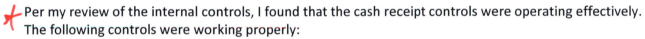

Check Date	Check number	Check Type	Amount	Payee	
12/1/20X2	4792	payment	$7,491.00	Mountain Dairy Company	C.4.8
12/3/20X2	4793	payment	$2,725.00	Denver Office Supplies	
12/4/20X2	4805	payment	$165.00	Cynthia Jamison, Attorney	
12/5/20X2	4815	payment	$4,284.00	Rocky Mountain Kitchen Goods	
12/28/20X2	4817	payment	$78,496.32	to Cash: Payroll Account	
12/30/20X2	4820	payment	$5,675.76	Milsap Foods	

Performed By: *ARO*　　　　　　　　　　　　　　　**Reviewed By:** *TES*
Date: *2/4/20X3*　　　　　　　　　　　　　　　　**Date:** *02/06/20X3*

Cash Disbursements TOC (continued):

Cash disbursement controls tested includes:

- The company employees follow the proper authorization limits where Miguel Lopez signs any checks under $5,000 and Alexis Madison co-signs (along with Miguel) any checks over $5,000.
- The company creates a voucher packet with the purchase order, vendor invoice, and the receiving report.
- The company cancels supporting documents with a PAID stamp, the date of payment, and the signature of the person signing the check.

Per review of the disbursement documents, the client's controls appear to be operating effectively.

Bank Reconciliation TOC:

During my testing of control procedures around the cash disbursements and cash receipts processes, I performed testing of control procedures on the bank reconciliation process. I obtained the October and November operating cash reconciliations. I reviewed the reconciliations and found that the following controls per the audit program were tested and found to be operating effectively.

Final Conclusion:
The controls over the cash receipts and cash disbursements processes are operating effectively.

Alpine Cupcakes, Inc.
Mailroom Control Listing
October 20X2

PBC

Created By: _____Diana Hayes_____   Date: __Daily Entries__

Reviewed By: _____Miguel Lopez_____   Date: __11/29/20X2__

Item No.	Date	Customer Name	Customer Number	Amount
1	10/1/20X2	Boulder Tea House	58300	$3.00
2	10/1/20X2	Broken Eggs Restaurant	62950	$3.00
3	10/1/20X2	Chavez Cantina	73678	$4,387.20
4	10/1/20X2	Denver Sirloin Restaurants	52058	$38.37
5	10/1/20X2	Elkhorn Coffee Shops	24701	$7,291.20
6	10/1/20X2	High Country Coffee	68752	$8,313.60
7	10/1/20X2	Nora's Café	67694	$5,248.80
8	10/1/20X2	Scotty's Taverns	43075	$19.53
9	10/1/20X2	Steinberg Delis	51535	$1,869.60
10	10/1/20X2	The Breakfast Place	50226	$33.93
11	10/1/20X2	UC Boulder Food Service	89500	$14,241.60
12	10/1/20X2	UC Denver Food Service	40669	$79.42
13	10/2/20X2	Country Barrel Restaurants	27978	$65.23
14	10/2/20X2	Granny's Café	40435	$33.47
15	10/2/20X2	Granny's Café	40435	$4,819.20
16	10/2/20X2	Steinberg Delis	51535	$12.98
17	10/2/20X2	The Breakfast Place	50226	$4,886.40
18	10/3/20X2	Brown's Tavern	31965	$484.80
19	10/3/20X2	Bubba's Fish House	53277	$787.20
20	10/3/20X2	Mile High Steakhouses	66286	$10,725.60
21	10/3/20X2	Smokey's Barbeque Pit	86485	$5,224.80
22	10/5/20X2	Luigi's Bistro	43288	$1,140.00
23	10/12/20X2	Elkhorn Coffee Shops	24701	$7,567.20
24	10/12/20X2	Luigi's Bistro	43288	$266.40
25	10/25/20X2	Little's Grill	18860	$7.18
26	10/25/20X2	Mountain Trout Fish House	72609	$5.80

Alpine Cupcakes, Inc.
Mailroom Control Listing
October 20X2

Performed by:
ARO 2/4/20X3
Reviewed by:
TES 02/06/20X3

Item No.	Date	Customer Name	Customer Number	Amount
27	10/25/20X2	Mountain Trout Fish House	72609	$835.20
28	10/25/20X2	Nora's Café	67694	$4,905.60
29	10/25/20X2	Smokey's Barbeque Pit	86485	$2,018.40
30	10/25/20X2	Southside Café	60445	$6.67
31	10/26/20X2	Boulder Tea House	58300	$285.60
32	10/26/20X2	Buckhead Restaurants	13438	$12.87
33	10/26/20X2	Pebbles Inn	75763	$864.00
34	10/26/20X2	St. Francis Hotel and Spa	46367	$4,216.80
35	10/26/20X2	UC Denver Food Service	40669	$60.20
36	10/27/20X2	Broken Eggs Restaurant	62950	$1,125.60
37	10/27/20X2	Chavez Cantina	73678	$26.08
38	10/27/20X2	Chavez Cantina	73678	$3,756.00
39	10/27/20X2	Denver Bakery Café	99242	$27.60
40	10/27/20X2	Granny's Café	40435	$22.47
41	10/27/20X2	Julie's Wraps	59316	$11.30
42	10/27/20X2	Julie's Wraps	59316	$1,627.20
43	10/27/20X2	Little's Grill	18860	$1,034.40
44	10/27/20X2	Nora's Café	67694	$24.13
45	10/28/20X2	Boulder Tea House	58300	$1.98
46	10/28/20X2	Bubba's Fish House	53277	$7.57
47	10/28/20X2	Elkhorn Coffee Shops	24701	$35.52
48	10/28/20X2	High Country Coffee	68752	$29.28
49	10/28/20X2	Steinberg Delis	51535	$1,180.80
50	10/28/20X2	The Sandwich Place	72927	$405.60
51	10/28/20X2	UC Boulder Food Service	89500	$10,154.40
52	10/29/20X2	Buckhead Restaurants	13438	$5,100.00
53	10/29/20X2	Mile High Steakhouses	66286	$63.20
54	10/29/20X2	Nora's Café	67694	$3,475.20
55	10/30/20X2	Brown's Tavern	31965	$645.60
56	10/30/20X2	Country Barrel Restaurants	27978	$41.82
57	10/30/20X2	Denver Sirloin Restaurants	52058	$33.33
58	10/30/20X2	Fontana Catering & Café	33692	$19.48

Client Supporting Document

Item No.	Date	Customer Name	Customer Number	Amount
59	10/30/20X2	Luigi's Bistro	43288	$15.45
60	10/30/20X2	Mountain Lion Restaurant	12295	$9.87
61	10/30/20X2	Pebbles Inn	75763	$6.00
62	10/30/20X2	Scotty's Taverns	43075	$9.82
63	10/30/20X2	Southside Café	60445	$960.00
64	10/30/20X2	The Breakfast Place	50226	$4,507.20
65	10/30/20X2	UC Boulder Food Service	89500	$70.52
66	10/31/20X2	Bon Appetito Restaurants	43754	$78.20
67	10/31/20X2	Broken Eggs Restaurant	62950	$3.00
68	10/31/20X2	Country Barrel Restaurants	27978	$6,021.60
69	10/31/20X2	Denver Sirloin Restaurants	52058	$4,800.00
70	10/31/20X2	High Country Coffee	68752	$4,216.80
71	10/31/20X2	Mile High Steakhouses	66286	$9,100.80
72	10/31/20X2	Papa's Restaurant	30700	$22.18
73	10/31/20X2	Smokey's Barbeque Pit	86485	$14.02
74	10/31/20X2	St. Francis Hotel and Spa	46367	$29.28
75	10/31/20X2	The Breakfast Place	50226	$31.30
76	10/31/20X2	The Sandwich Place	72927	$2.82
77	10/31/20X2	UC Denver Food Service	40669	$8,668.80
78				
79				
80				

Monthly Reconciliation:

Total Received—October 20X2	158,177.07
Total per the Cash Receipts Journal	188,177.07
Subtract Storefront Cash Receipts	30,000.00
Total Customer Receipts per General Ledger	158,177.07
Difference:	0.00

Signature of Reconciler: _____Lindsay McKenna_____   Date: 11/12/2X2

PBC

Created By: _____ Diana Hayes _____   Date: _Daily Entries_

Reviewed By: ___ Miguel Lopez ___   Date: _1/5/20X3_

Item No.	Date	Customer Name	Customer Number	Amount
1	12/1/20X2	Country Barrel Restaurants	27978	$6,933.60
2	12/1/20X2	Mountain Trout Fish House	72609	$15.97
3	12/1/20X2	Mountain Trout Fish House	72609	$2,299.20
4	12/1/20X2	Southside Café	60445	$20.13
5	12/1/20X2	St. Francis Hotel and Spa	46367	$2,047.20
6	12/1/20X2	UC Boulder Food Service	89500	$11,455.20
7	12/2/20X2	Bon Appetito Restaurants	43754	$10,968.00
8	12/2/20X2	Brown's Tavern	31965	$547.20
9	12/2/20X2	High Country Coffee	68752	$4,852.80
10	12/2/20X2	Scotty's Taverns	43075	$10.07
11	12/2/20X2	St. Francis Hotel and Spa	46367	$14.22
12	12/2/20X2	Steinberg Delis	51535	$7.32
13	12/2/20X2	Steinberg Delis	51535	$1,053.60
14	12/2/20X2	The Sandwich Place	72927	$1,221.60
15	12/2/20X2	UC Denver Food Service	40669	$8,450.40
16	12/3/20X2	Broken Eggs Restaurant	62950	$1,063.20
17	12/3/20X2	Denver Bakery Café	99242	$5,284.80
18	12/3/20X2	Granny's Café	40435	$2,620.80
19	12/3/20X2	Smokey's Barbeque Pit	86485	$4,440.00
20	12/13/20X2	Bon Appetito Restaurants	43754	$15,040.80
21	12/13/20X2	Elkhorn Coffee Shops	24701	$7,972.80
22	12/18/20X2	Bon Appetito Restaurants	43754	$11,260.80
23	12/24/20X2	Bon Appetito Restaurants	43754	$13,161.60
24	12/25/20X2	Bon Appetito Restaurants	43754	$94.45
25	12/25/20X2	Chavez Cantina	73678	$28.33
26	12/25/20X2	Granny's Café	40435	$22.30

Performed by:
ARO 2/4/20X3
Reviewed by:
TES 02/06/20X3

Item No.	Date	Customer Name	Customer Number	Amount
27	12/25/20X2	Mile High Steakhouses	66286	$63.60
28	12/25/20X2	Scotty's Taverns	43075	$2.57
29	12/26/20X2	Bon Appetito Restaurants	43754	$13,600.80
30	12/26/20X2	Broken Eggs Restaurant	62950	$12.18
31	12/26/20X2	Buckhead Restaurants	13438	$27.53
32	12/26/20X2	Chavez Cantina	73678	$4,080.00
33	12/26/20X2	Country Barrel Restaurants	27978	$7,180.80
34	12/26/20X2	High Country Coffee	68752	$6,566.40
35	12/26/20X2	Julie's Wraps	59316	$16.77
36	12/26/20X2	Luigi's Bistro	43288	$16.53
37	12/26/20X2	Mountain Lion Restaurant	12295	$3,520.80
38	12/26/20X2	Papa's Restaurant	30700	$2,611.20
39	12/26/20X2	Smokey's Barbeque Pit	86485	$29.05
40	12/26/20X2	St. Francis Hotel and Spa	46367	$1,840.80
41	12/27/20X2	Boulder Tea House	58300	$3.33
42	12/27/20X2	Bubba's Fish House	53277	$17.38
43	12/27/20X2	Bubba's Fish House	53277	$2,503.20
44	12/27/20X2	Elkhorn Coffee Shops	24701	$41.43
45	12/27/20X2	Mountain Trout Fish House	72609	$16.15
46	12/27/20X2	Nora's Café	67694	$33.97
47	12/27/20X2	Southside Café	60445	$2,757.60
48	12/27/20X2	UC Boulder Food Service	89500	$79.65
49	12/27/20X2	UC Denver Food Service	40669	$61.27
50	12/28/20X2	Brown's Tavern	31965	$1.67
51	12/28/20X2	Country Barrel Restaurants	27978	$49.87
52	12/28/20X2	Denver Sirloin Restaurants	52058	$24.55
53	12/28/20X2	Fontana Catering & Café	33692	$16.48
54	12/28/20X2	Little's Grill	18860	$6.53
55	12/28/20X2	Mountain Lion Restaurant	12295	$24.45
56	12/28/20X2	Mountain Trout Fish House	72609	$2,325.60
57	12/28/20X2	Nora's Café	67694	$4,560.00
58	12/28/20X2	Papa's Restaurant	30700	$18.13

Client Supporting Document

C.2.3: pg. 2 of 3

Alpine Cupcakes, Inc.
Mailroom Control Listing
December 20X2

Item No.	Date	Customer Name	Customer Number	Amount
59	12/28/20X2	Pebbles Inn	75763	$3.10
60	12/28/20X2	Southside Café	60445	$19.15
61	12/28/20X2	St. Francis Hotel and Spa	46367	$12.78
62	12/28/20X2	Steinberg Delis	51535	$12.18
63	12/28/20X2	The Breakfast Place	50226	$28.75
64	12/28/20X2	The Sandwich Place	72927	$11.05
65	12/29/20X2	Fontana Catering & Café	33692	$2,373.60
66	12/29/20X2	Granny's Café	40435	$3,211.20
67	12/30/20X2	Julie's Wraps	59316	$2,414.40
68	12/30/20X2	The Breakfast Place	50226	$4,140.00
69	12/30/20X2	UC Boulder Food Service	89500	$11,469.60
70	12/30/20X2	UC Denver Food Service	40669	$8,822.40
71	12/31/20X2	Boulder Tea House	58300	$480.00
72	12/31/20X2	Broken Eggs Restaurant	62950	$1,754.40
73				
74				
75				
76				
77				
78				
79				
80				

Monthly Reconciliation:

Total Received—December 20X2	197,749.29
Total per the Cash Receipts Journal	227,749.29
Subtract Storefront Cash Receipts	0.00
Total Customer Receipts per the General Ledger	227,749.29
Difference:	(30,000.00)

Signature of Reconciler: _____Lindsay McKenna_____   Date:_01/10/20X3

Performed by:
ARO 2/4/20X3
Reviewed by:
TES 02/06/20X3

Alpine Cupcakes, Inc. Check Copy

ALPINE CUPCAKES, INC.   **COPY**
1250 16th Street
Denver, Colorado 80202   Check No.   4792
                                             Date   12/1/20X2

** Seven Thousand Four Hundred Ninety One and 00/100 Dollars $7,491.00

Mountain Dairy Company
450 25th Street
Greeley, CO 80631

Authorized Signature: *Miguel Lopez*
                         Alexis Madison

ALPINE CUPCAKES, INC.

Mountain Dairy Company	12/1/20X2		Check No: 4792
Discount	Amount Paid	Discount	Amount Paid
	$7,491.00		
		Total	$7,491.00

**PAID
12/1/20X2**

Miguel Lopez

Performed by:
ARO 2/4/20X3
Reviewed by:
TES 02/06/20X3

Mountain Dairy Sales Invoice

Mountain Dairy Company
450 25th Street
Greeley, CO 80631
Contact: Steve Brohmel

Date: 11/2/20X2
Due Date: 12/2/20X2

Ship To:
Alpine Cupcakes, Inc.
1250 16th Street
Denver, Colorado 80202

Bill To:
Same as Shipping Address

Invoice No: 00025777
Sales Order Number: 00026810

Customer PO Number: 6700
Purchase Order Date: 10/17/20X2

Ordered	Quantity Back Ordered	Shipped	Unit	Description	Unit Price	Total
13		13	gallons	Almond milk	$4.00	$52.00
1642		1642	pounds	Butter	$2.00	$3,284.00
32		32	gallons	Cream	$10.00	$320.00
272		272	pounds	Cream cheese	$5.00	$1,360.00
920		920	dozen	Eggs	$1.50	$1,380.00
157		157	gallons	Milk	$3.00	$471.00
272		272	pounds	Sour cream	$2.00	$544.00
20		20	gallons	Vanilla soymilk	$4.00	$80.00

**PAID
12/1/20X2**

Miguel Lopez

Shipment Total	$7,491.00
Sales Tax	N/A
Freight	N/A
Invoice Total	$7,491.00

Alpine Cupcakes Purchase Order

Alpine Cupcakes, Inc.
1250 16th Street
Denver, Colorado 80202

Order No.:	6700
Date:	10/17/20X2
Page	1
Ship Date:	11/2/20X2

Purchased From:
Mountain Dairy Company
450 25th Street
Greeley, CO 80631

Ship To:
Alpine Cupcakes, Inc.
1250 16th Street
Denver, Colorado 80202

Ordered	Unit	Description	Tax	Unit Price	Total
13	gallons	Almond milk		$4.00	$52.00
1642	pounds	Butter		$2.00	$3,284.00
32	gallons	Cream		$10.00	$320.00
272	pounds	Cream cheese		$5.00	$1,360.00
920	dozen	Eggs		$1.50	$1,380.00
157	gallons	Milk		$3.00	$471.00
272	pounds	Sour cream		$2.00	$544.00
20	gallons	Vanilla soymilk		$4.00	$80.00

Shipped By: Mountain Dairy Company

Purchase Approved By: *Priscilla Orr*

Purchase Approval Date: __10/17/20x2__

Total Amount $7,491.00

**PAID
12/1/20X2**

Miguel Lopez

Alpine Cupcakes, Inc.
Mountain Dairy Company Voucher Packet

Performed by:
ARO 2/4/20X3
Reviewed by:
TES 02/06/20X3

ALPINE CUPCAKES, INC.

Receiving Report

Date: _11/2/20x2_

Purchase Order #: ___6700___   Receiving Report #: ___11159___

Received From: _Mountain Dairy Company_

Freight Carrier: _Mountain Dairy Company_

Quantity	Unit	Description
13	gallons	almond milk
1642	pounds	butter
32	gallons	cream
272	pounds	cream cheese
920	dozen	eggs
157	gallons	milk
272	pounds	sour cream
20	gallons	vanilla soymilk

Remarks: ___Items received in OK condition___

Received By: ___Gabrielle Krause___

Delivered To: ___Receiving Dept.___

**PAID
12/1/20X2**

Miguel Lopez

Performed by:
ARO 2/4/20X3
Reviewed by:
TES 02/06/20X3

Alpine Cupcakes, Inc. Check Copy

ALPINE CUPCAKES, INC.   **COPY**
1250 16th Street
Denver, Colorado 80202   Check No.   4793
                                                Date   12/1/20X2

**Two Thousand Seven Hundred Twenty Five and 00/100 Dollars $2,725.00

Denver Office Supplies
9000 E Hampden Avenue
Denver, CO 80202

Authorized Signature: *Miguel Lopez*

Alexis Madison

ALPINE CUPCAKES, INC.

Denver Office Supplies	12/1/20X2			Check No: 4793
Discount	Amount Paid	Discount		Amount Paid
	$ 2,725.00			
			Total	$2,725.00

Denver Office Supplies
9000 E Hampden Avenue
Denver, CO 80202
Sales Invoice

Invoice No: 111664
Date: 12/03/20x2
Due Date: 01/03/20x2
Contact: Jan Ingrams

Customer PO Number: 6725
Purchase Order Date: 12/03/20x2

Ship To:

Alpine Cupcakes, Inc.
1250 16th Street
Denver, Colorado 80202

Bill To:
Same as Shipping
Address

Unit	Unit Price	Description	Total
100	$4.99	printer paper	$499.00
100	$3.59	writing pads	$359.00
100	$2.50	pens	$250.00
100	$1.99	pencils	$199.00
100	$2.18	folders/binders/notebooks	$218.00
2	$500.00	printers	$1,000.00
2	$100.00	phones	$200.00

Shipment Total	$2,725.00
Sales Tax	N/A
Freight	N/A
Invoice Total	$2,725.00

Performed by:
ARO 2/4/20X3
Reviewed by:
TES 02/06/20X3

Alpine Cupcakes Purchase Order

Alpine Cupcakes, Inc.
1250 16th Street
Denver, Colorado 80202

Order No.:	6725
Date:	12/3/20X2
Page	1
Ship Date:	12/3/20X2

Purchased From:
Denver Office Supplies
9000 E Hampden Avenue
Denver, CO 80202

Ship To:
Alpine Cupcakes, Inc.
1250 16th Street
Denver, Colorado 80202

Ordered	Unit	Description	Tax	Unit Price	Total
100	1	printer paper		$4.99	$499.00
100	1	writing pads		$3.59	$359.00
100	1	pens		$2.50	$250.00
100	1	pencils		$1.99	$199.00
100	1	folders/binders/notebooks		$2.18	$218.00
2	1	printers		$500.00	$1,000.00
2	1	phones		$100.00	$200.00

Shipped By: Denver Office Supplies

Purchase Approved By: *Priscilla Orr*

Purchase Approval Date: __12/03/20x2__

Total Amount $2,725.00

Alpine Cupcakes, Inc.
Denver Office Supplies Voucher Packet

Performed by:
ARO 2/4/20X3
Reviewed by:
TES 02/06/20X3

ALPINE CUPCAKES, INC.
Receiving Report

Date: 12/3/20x2

Purchase Order #: 6725

Received From: Denver Office Supplies

Freight Carrier: Denver Office Supplies

Receiving Report #: 11169

Quantity	Unit	Description
100	1	printer paper
100	1	writing pads
100	1	pens
100	1	pencils
100	1	folders/binders/notebooks
2	1	printer
2	1	phones

Remarks: Items received in OK condition

Received By: Gabrielle Krause

Delivered To: Receiving Dept.

Performed by:
ARO 2/4/20X3
Reviewed by:
TES 02/06/20X3

Alpine Cupcakes, Inc. Check Copy

ALPINE CUPCAKES, INC.
1250 16th Street
Denver, Colorado 80202

COPY

Check No.	4805
Date	12/4/20X2

** One Hundred Sixty Five and 00/100 Dollars $165.00

Cynthia Jamison
65 S. Cherry St. Suite 1000
Denver, CO 80202

Authorized Signature: *Diana Hayes*

ALPINE CUPCAKES, INC.

Cynthia Jamison	12/4/20X2		Check No: 4805
Discount	Amount Paid	Discount	Amount Paid
	$165.00		
		Total	$165.00

**PAID
12/4/20X2**

Miguel Lopez

Cynthia Jamison, Attorney
Sales Invoice

Our Company Address: 65 S. Cherry St. Suite 1000
                          Denver, CO 80202

Client Information: Alpine Cupcakes, Inc.
Client Address: 1250 16th St.
                  Denver, Colorado 80202

Invoice #:   2437
Invoice Date: 11/05/20X2

Description:
Monthly attorney fees for legal expertise

Monthly Service Hours	Rate per Hour		Total
2	$ 82.50	$	165.00

**PAID
12/4/20X2**

Miguel Lopez

Performed by:
ARO 2/4/20X3
Reviewed by:
TES 02/06/20X3

Alpine Cupcakes, Inc. Check Copy

ALPINE CUPCAKES, INC.   **COPY**
1250 16th Street
Denver, Colorado 80202   Check No.   4815
                                                Date   12/5/20X2

**Four Thousand Two Hundred Eighty Four and 00/100 Dollars $4,284.00

Rocky Mountain Kitchen Goods
1212 S. Broadway
Denver, CO 80202

                    Authorized Signature: *Miguel Lopez*
                                               Alexis Madison

---

ALPINE CUPCAKES, INC.

Rocky Mountain Kitchen Goods	12/5/20X2		Check No: 4815
Discount	Amount Paid	Discount	Amount Paid
	$4,284.00		
		Total	$4,284.00

**PAID
12/5/20X2**

Miguel Lopez

| Performed by: |
| ARO 2/4/20X3 |
| Reviewed by: |
| TES 02/06/20X3 |

Rocky Mountain Kitchen Goods
Sales Invoice

1212 S. Broadway
Denver, CO 80202
Contact: Stephanie
Simpson

Date: 11/5/20X2
Due Date: 12/5/20X2

Ship and Bill To:
Alpine Cupcakes, Inc.
1250 16th Street
Denver, Colorado 80202

Invoice No: 10298
Sales Order Number:
12662

Customer PO
Number: 6726

Purchase Order Date: 10/5/20X2

Quantity Ordered	Back Ordered	Shipped	Description	Unit Price	Total
25		25	cooking utensils	$17.00	$425.00
30		30	cooking utensils	$22.00	$660.00
15		15	cooking utensils	$69.00	$1,035.00
35		35	cooking supplies	$45.00	$1,575.00
20		20	cooking pans	$25.00	$500.00
10		10	towels	$6.00	$60.00
10		10	hot pads	$2.50	$25.00
1		1	measuring cups	$4.00	$4.00

Shipment Total	$4,284.00
Sales Tax	N/A
Freight	N/A
Invoice Total	$4,284.00

**PAID
12/5/20X2**

Miguel Lopez

Alpine Cupcakes, Inc.
Rocky Mountain Kitchen Goods Voucher Packet

Alpine Cupcakes Purchase Order

Alpine Cupcakes, Inc.
1250 16th Street
Denver, Colorado 80202

Order No.:	6726
Date:	10/5/20X2
Page	1
Ship Date:	11/5/20X2

Purchased From:
Rocky Mountain Kitchen Goods
1212 S. Broadway
Denver, CO 80202

Ship To:
Alpine Cupcakes, Inc.
1250 16th Street
Denver, Colorado 80202

Ordered	Unit	Description	Tax	Unit Price	Total
25		cooking utensils		$17.00	$425.00
30		cooking utensils		$22.00	$660.00
15		cooking utensils		$69.00	$1,035.00
35		cooking supplies		$45.00	$1,575.00
20		cooking pans		$25.00	$500.00
10		towels		$6.00	$60.00
10		hot pads		$2.50	$25.00
1		measuring cups		$4.00	$4.00

Shipped By: Rocky Mountain Kitchen Goods

Purchase Approved By: *Priscilla Orr*

Purchase Approval Date: *11/06/20x2*

Total Amount $4,284.00

PAID
12/5/20X2

Miguel Lopez

Performed by:
ARO 2/4/20X3
Reviewed by:
TES 02/06/20X3

Alpine Cupcakes, Inc. Check Copy

ALPINE CUPCAKES, INC.	**COPY**
1250 16th Street	
Denver, Colorado 80202	

	Check No.	4820
	Date	12/30/20X2

** Five Thousand Six Hundred Seventy Five and 76/100 Dollars $5,675.76

Milsap Foods
24377 NE Airport Road
Aurora, OR 97002

Authorized Signature: *Miguel Lopez*
                          Diana Hayes

ALPINE CUPCAKES, INC.

Milsap Foods		12/30/20X2			Check No: 4820
Discount	Amount Paid		Discount		mount Paid
	$5,675.76				
				Total	$5,675.76

PAID
12/30/20X2

Miguel Lopez

Client Supporting Document

C.2.8: pg. 1 of 4

74

Performed by:
ARO 2/4/20X3
Reviewed by:
TES 02/06/20X3

Milsap Foods Sales Invoice

Milsap Foods
24377 NE Airport Road
Aurora, OR 97002
Contact: Isabella Hernandez

Date: 12/03/20x2
Due Date: 1/2/20x2

Ship To:
Alpine Cupcakes, Inc.
1250 16th Street
Denver, Colorado 80202

Bill To:
Same as Shipping Address

Invoice No: 4172
Sales Order Number: 4388

Customer PO No: 6710
PO Date: 11/15/20x2

Ordered	Quantity Back Ordered	Shipped	Unit	Description	Unit Price	Total
25		25	pounds	Baking powder	$ 3.00	$ 75.00
10		10	pounds	Baking soda	$ 1.40	$ 14.00
2		2	quarts	Cider vinegar	$ 3.00	$ 6.00
6		6	gallons	Coconut oil	$ 20.00	$ 120.00
5,316		5,316	pounds	Confectioners' sugar	$ 0.56	$ 2,976.96
68		68	pounds	Cornstarch	$ 4.00	$ 272.00
1,676		1,676	pounds	Flour	$ 0.30	$ 502.80
29		29	pounds	Millet flour	$ 3.00	$ 87.00
89		89	pounds	Rice flour	$ 1.20	$ 106.80
12		12	pounds	Salt	$ 0.20	$ 2.40
576		576	pounds	Shortening	$ 0.55	$ 316.80
2,128		2,128	pounds	Sugar	$ 0.50	$ 1,064.00
33		33	gallons	Vegetable Oil	$ 4.00	$ 132.00

Shipment Total	$5,675.76
Sales Tax	N/A
Freight	N/A
Invoice Total	$5,675.76

PAID
12/30/20X2

Miguel Lopez

Performed by:
ARO 2/4/20X3
Reviewed by:
TES 02/06/20X3

Alpine Cupcakes Purchase Order

Alpine Cupcakes, Inc.
1250 16th Street
Denver, Colorado 80202

Order No.:	6710
Date:	11/15/20X2
Page	1
Ship Date:	12/03/20X2

Purchased From:
Milsap Foods
24377 NE Airport Road
Aurora, OR 97002

Ship To:
Alpine Cupcakes, Inc.
1250 16th Street
Denver, Colorado 80202

Ordered	Unit	Description	Tax	Unit Price	Total
25	pounds	Baking powder		$ 3.00	$ 75.00
10	pounds	Baking soda		$ 1.40	$ 14.00
2	Quart	Cider vinegar		$ 3.00	$ 6.00
6	gallons	Coconut oil		$ 20.00	$ 120.00
5,316	pounds	Confectioners' sugar		$ 0.56	$ 2,976.96
68	pounds	Cornstarch		$ 4.00	$ 272.00
1,676	pounds	Flour		$ 0.30	$ 502.80
29	pounds	Millet flour		$ 3.00	$ 87.00
89	pounds	Rice flour		$ 1.20	$ 106.80
12	pounds	Salt		$ 0.20	$ 2.40
576	pounds	Shortening		$ 0.55	$ 316.80
2,128	pounds	Sugar		$ 0.50	$ 1,064.00
33	gallons	Vegetable Oil		$ 4.00	$ 132.00

Purchase Approved By: *Priscilla Orr*

Purchase Approval Date: *11/18/20x2*

Total Amount $ 5,675.76

PAID
12/30/20X2

Miguel Lopez

Performed by:
ARO 2/4/20X3
Reviewed by:
TES 02/06/20X3

ALPINE CUPCAKES, INC.
Receiving Report

Date: 12/03/20x2

Purchase Order #: 6710

Received From: Milsap Foods

Freight Carrier: Milsap Foods

Receiving Report #: 11168

Quantity	Unit	Description
25	pounds	baking powder
10	pounds	baking soda
2	quarts	cider vinegar
6	gallons	coconut oil
5,316	pounds	confectioners' sugar
68	pounds	cornstarch
1,676	pounds	flour
29	pounds	millet flour
89	pounds	rice flour
12	pounds	salt
576	pounds	shortening
2,128	pounds	sugar
33	gallons	vegetable oil

Remarks: Items received in OK condition

Received By: Gabrielle Krause

Delivered To: Receiving Dept.

PAID
12/30/20X2

Miguel Lopez

Alpine Cupcakes, Inc.
Payroll Transfer Voucher Packet

Performed by:
ARO 2/4/20X3
Reviewed by:
TES 02/06/20X3

Alpine Cupcakes, Inc. Check Copy

ALPINE CUPCAKES, INC.	**COPY**
1250 16th Street	
Denver, Colorado 80202	Check No. 4817
	Date 12/1/20X2

**Seventy Eight Four Hundred Ninety Six and 32/100 Dollars $ 78,496.32

Cash: Payroll Account
ALPINE CUPCAKES, INC.
1250 16th Street
Denver, Colorado 80202   Authorized Signature: _Miguel Lopez_____

ALPINE CUPCAKES, INC.

Cash: Payroll Account		12/1/20X2		Check No: 4817
Discount	Amount Paid	Discount		Amount Paid
	$ 78,496.32			
			Total	$78,496.32

**PAID
12/28/20X2**

Miguel Lopez

Performed by:
ARO 2/4/20X3
Reviewed by:
TES 02/06/20X3

PBC

Prepared By:___Lindsay McKenna_____   Date: _11/06/20X2_

Reviewed By: ___Miguel Lopez_____   Date: _11/10/20X2_

Balance per GL:	$349,819.43		Balance per Bank Statement	$374,301.27
Add:			Add:	
			Deposits in Transit	81,123.04
Subtract:			Subtract:	
New Check Fee	(50.00)		Outstanding Checks	(105,661.88)
Monthly Service Fee	(25.00)			
			Unreconcilable Difference	(18.00)
Corrected Cash Balance	$349,744.43		Corrected Cash Balance	$349,744.43

PBC

Prepared By: _Diana Hayes_   Date: _12/10/20X2_

Reviewed By: _Miguel Lopez_   Date: _12/21/20X2_

Balance per GL:	$336,733.09	Balance per Bank Statement	$400,709.08
Add:		Add:	
		Deposits in Transit	34,603.86
Subtract:		Subtract:	
Monthly Service Fee	(25.00)	Outstanding Checks	(98,572.85)
		Unreconcilable Difference	(32.00)
Corrected Cash Balance	$336,708.09	Corrected Cash Balance	$336,708.09

Alpine Cupcakes, Inc.
Cash Confirmation Memo
Audit Year December 31, 20X2

Garcia and Foster, CPAs

Performed By: *ARO*   **Reviewed By:** *TES*
Date: *1/18/20X3*   **Date:** *01/24/20X3*

I reviewed the trial balance to identify the material cash balances. Any balances greater than TM ($3,700) are deemed to be material. The following balances as of 12/31/20X3 were deemed to be material:

	Description	Account No.	Amount
1.	Cash—Storefront	1100	$ 124,473.95
2.	Cash—Corporate	1101	441,786.75
3.	Cash—Payroll	1102	123,227.85

Once these accounts were identified, I asked Miguel Lopez to create a cash confirmation to be sent to the Bank of Boulder. Miguel inputted the bank and account information. Then he signed and dated the confirmation form. Once the form was completed, we obtained the form and made a copy. Then Miguel Lopez sent the original confirmation to the bank for us. We gave him a self-addressed envelope to our accounting office to be included with the signed confirmation. The following cash confirmation control listing was completed:

Account No.	Bank Account No.	Description	1st Date Sent	2nd Date Sent	Date Received	TB Amount	Bank Amount
1100	7934501	Storefront	1/03/20X3		1/12/20X3	124,473.95	150,856.34
1101	5409826	Corporate	1/03/20X3		1/12/20X3	441,786.75	464,118.20
1102	6193074	Payroll	1/03/20X3		1/12/20X3	123,227.85	101,147.49

Final Conclusion:
Per my review of the cash confirmation documentation, there were no issues found in the confirmation process. See C.3.3 and C.4.1 for more details.

| Performed by: |
| Reviewed by: |

Alpine Cupcakes, Inc.
Customer Name

We have provided to our accountants the following information as of the close of business on **December 31, 20X2**, regarding our deposit and loan balances. Please confirm the accuracy of the information, noting any exceptions to the information provided. If the balances have been left blank, please complete this form by furnishing the balance in the appropriate space below. *Although we do not request nor expect you to conduct a comprehensive, detailed search of your records, if during the process of completing this confirmation additional information about other deposit and loan accounts we may have with you comes to your attention, please include such information below. Please use the enclosed envelope to return the form directly to our auditors.

Financial Institution's Name and Address

[ ]
Bank of Boulder
1573 Market Street
Denver, CO 80202
[ ]

1. At the close of business on the date listed above, our records indicated the following deposit balance(s):

Account Name	Account No.	Interest Rate	Balance*
Cash: Storefront	7934501		
Cash: Corporate Accounts	5409826		
Cash: Payroll	6193074		

2. We were directly liable to the financial institution for loans at the close of business on the date listed above as follows:

Account No./ Description	Balance	Date Due	Interest Rate	Date Through Which Interest Is Paid	Description of Collateral

Miguel Lopez   _1/03/20X3_
(Customer's Authorized Signature)   (Date)

The information presented above by the customer is in agreement with our records. Although we have not conducted a comprehensive, detailed search of our records, no other deposit or loan accounts have come to our attention except as noted below.

_____   _____
(Financial Institution Authorized Signature)   (Date)

_____
(Title)

Exceptions and/or Comments

Please return this form directly to our accountants:

[Garcia and Foster, CPAs
1790 Lawrence Street
Denver, CO 80202   ]

*Ordinarily, balances are left blank intentionally.

Garcia and Foster Audit Workpaper   C.3.2: pg. 1 of 1

Performed by:
ARO 1/18/20X3
Reviewed by:

**RECEIVED BY
ALPINE
CUPCAKES, INC.
JAN 17 20X2**

Alpine Cupcakes, Inc.
Customer Name

We have provided to our accountants the following information as of the close of business on **December 31, 20X2**, regarding our deposit and loan balances. Please confirm the accuracy of the information, noting any exceptions to the information provided. If the balances have been left blank, please complete this form by furnishing the balance in the appropriate space below. *Although we do not request nor expect you to conduct a comprehensive, detailed search of your records, if during the process of completing this confirmation additional information about other deposit and loan accounts we may have with you comes to your attention, please include such information below. Please use the enclosed envelope to return the form directly to our auditors.

Financial
Institution's
Name and
Address

[
Bank of Boulder
1573 Market Street
Denver, CO 80202
]

3. At the close of business on the date listed above, our records indicated the following deposit balance(s):

Account Name	Account No.	Interest Rate	Balance*
Cash: Storefront	7934501	*None*	*$150,856.34*
Cash: Corporate Accounts	5409826	*None*	*$464,118.20*
Cash: Payroll	6193074	*None*	*$101,147.49*

4. We were directly liable to the financial institution for loans at the close of business on the date listed above as follows:

Account No./ Description	Balance	Date Due	Interest Rate	Date through which interest is paid	Description of Collateral
Note Payable — Chevy Van	*$35,393.70*	*12/31/20X7*	*5%*	*12/31/20X2*	*Chevy Van*

_____*Miguel Lopez*_____   _____*1/03/20X3*_____
(Customer's Authorized Signature)   (Date)

The information presented above by the customer is in agreement with our records. Although we have not conducted a comprehensive, detailed search of our records, no other deposit or loan accounts have come to our attention except as noted below.

_____*Susan Roberts*_____   _____*1/9/20X3*_____
(Financial Institution Authorized Signature)   (Date)
_____*Bank Manager*_____
(Title)

Exceptions and/or Comments
The company's cash is restricted. The mortgage includes debt covenants that require the company to maintain a daily cash balance of $200,000 in the storefront bank account.

Please return this form directly to our accountants:

[
Garcia and Foster, CPAs
1790 Lawrence Street
Denver, CO 80202
]

*Ordinarily, balances are left blank intentionally.

Garcia and Foster Audit Workpaper

C.3.3: pg. 1 of 1

Alpine Cupcakes, Inc.
Bank Reconciliation Memo
December 31, 20X2

Garcia and Foster, CPAs

Performed By: *ARO*   **Reviewed By:** *TES*
Date: *2/8/20X3*   **Date:** *02/14/20X3*

I performed substantive testing of cash balances. I obtained the December bank reconciliation for the corporate cash account from Lindsay McKenna. In addition, Lindsay provided me with the November and December outstanding check listings, as well as the December and January bank statements.

Reconciliation of the Outstanding Check List:

Ending November O/S check balance:	$ 98,572.85	C.4.6
Add: December Checks Written	128,669.03	C.4.8
Subtract: Checks Clearing in December	(127,099.14)	C.4.4
Balance	100,142.74	
Balance per December O/S Check Listing	105,132.74	C.4.3
Difference	$ 4,990.00	*immaterial difference*

Per my review of the bank reconciliation documentation, there were no issues found in the bank reconciliation process and the ending cash balance for 20X2. These procedures validate the existence and rights to the asset assertions. See C.4.1 to C.4.8 for more details.

Final Conclusion on Cash Account:
Based upon my work, I believe the cash balance is fairly stated.

Performed by:
ARO 2/8/20X3
Reviewed by:
TES 02/14/20X3

PBC

Prepared By: ___Lindsay McKenna___   Date: _1/07/20X3_

Reviewed By: ___*Miguel Lopez*___   Date: _1/12/20X3_

Balance per GL:	$441,786.75	*TB*	Balance per Bank Statement	$469,108.20	
Add:			Add:		
Interest Earned	100.00	*3*	Deposits in Transit	77,746.29	*2*
Subtract:			Subtract:		
New Check Fee	(50.00)	*i*	Outstanding Checks	(105,132.74)	*1*
Monthly Service Fee	(25.00)	*i*			
			Unreconcilable Difference	90.00	*i*
Corrected Cash Balance	$441,811.75		Corrected Cash Balance	$441,811.75	

Tickmark Legend:

TB - Agreed to November Trial Balance.

1 - Agreed to O/S Check Listing at C.4.6

2 - Agreed to Deposit in Transit Listing at C.4.3

3 - Tied information to the December Bank Statement at C.4.4

F - Footed.

i - immaterial

Performed by:
ARO 2/8/20X3
Reviewed by:
TES 02/14/20X3

PBC

Operating Outstanding Check Listing
Dec. 31, 20X2

Date	Check Number	Payee	Outstanding Check Amount	
01/04/20X1	4017	Summit Cleaners	$ 145.00	
03/04/20X1	4077	U.S. Post Office	40.50	
04/04/20X1	4118	Cynthia Jamison, Attorney	153.00	
08/04/20X1	4254	Garcia & Foster CPAs	272.50	
09/04/20X1	4279	Joe's Organic Supplies	76.00	
10/04/20X1	4330	Republic Waste Services	50.00	
12/04/20X1	4398	Republic Waste Services	50.00	
01/04/20X2	4437	Speedy Fountain Service	408.00	
03/29/20X2	4508	PaperMart	1,186.00	
04/04/20X2	4539	City of Denver	136.25	
06/04/20X2	4593	Farmers Insurance	404.80	
08/04/20X2	4670	Summit Cleaners	127.60	
09/04/20X2	4698	Qwest Telephone	154.50	
10/31/20X2	4756	Boulder Spice Importers	2,579.40	
11/04/20X2	4777	Republic Waste Services	50.00	
12/04/20X2	4812	Jerry's Handiman	111.25	
12/28/20X2	4819	PaperMart	1,747.00	Υ
12/30/20X2	4820	Milsap Foods	5,675.76	Υ
12/31/20X2	4821	Colorado Dept. of Revenue	1,446.18	Υ
12/28/20X2	4817	to Cash: Payroll Account	78,496.32	Υ
12/28/20X2	4818	Mountain Dairy Company	10,376.50	Υ
12/31/20X2	4822	Denver City Dept. of Revenue	1,446.18	Υ
		Total O/S checks December	$ 105,132.74	C.4.1
			F	

Operating Deposits in Transit
Dec. 31, 20X2

Date	Payee	Amount
12/28/20X2	Daily Bank Deposit	$ 37,114.29
12/29/20X2	Daily Bank Deposit	5,584.80
12/30/20X2	Daily Bank Deposit	26,846.40
12/31/20X2	Daily Bank Deposit	8,200.80
	Total DIT—Dec.	$ 77,746.29
		F

F - Footed.

Υ - Traced to clearance on January Bank Statement at C.4.6

Performed by:
Reviewed by:

Bank of Boulder

1573 Market Street
Denver, CO 80202

Alpine Cupcakes, Inc.
1250 16th Street
Denver, Colorado 80202

December 1, 20X2 through December 31, 20X2

Account Number:	5409826

CUSTOMER SERVICE INFORMATION

Service Center:	1-800-555-8342
Hearing Impaired:	1-800-555-3422
Para Española:	1-800-555-1600
International Calls:	1-208-555-1212

CHECKING SUMMARY

	AMOUNT
Beginning Balance	$ 400,709.08
Deposits and Additions	190,583.26
Checks Paid	127,099.14
Bank Charges	75.00
Ending Balance	$ 464,118.20

CHECKS PAID

CHECK NUMBER	DATE PAID	AMOUNT
4784	12/01/20X2	$ 76,581.10
4785	12/06/20X2	1,182.24
4792	12/06/20X2	7,491.00
4786	12/07/20X2	1,182.23
4806	12/07/20X2	444.00
4808	12/07/20X2	275.00
4814	12/07/20X2	456.00
4791	12/08/20X2	424.00
4805	12/08/20X2	165.00
4807	12/08/20X2	123.25
4783	12/09/20X2	1,466.50
4788	12/09/20X2	7,140.00
4789	12/09/20X2	1,745.00
4790	12/09/20X2	467.00
4794	12/09/20X2	2,657.80
4796	12/09/20X2	345.00
4809	12/09/20X2	1,584.00
4815	12/09/20X2	4,284.00
4793	12/10/20X2	2,725.00
4802	12/10/20X2	50.40

Performed by:

Reviewed by:

CHECKS PAID (continued)

CHECK NUMBER	DATE PAID	AMOUNT
4803	12/10/20X2	265.00
4787	12/11/20X2	4,565.63
4804	12/11/20X2	270.00
9132	12/11/20X2	4,990.00
4795	12/12/20X2	2,700.00
4811	12/12/20X2	348.54
4813	12/12/20X2	143.75
4798	12/13/20X2	800.00
4799	12/13/20X2	426.80
4801	12/13/20X2	345.00
4797	12/14/20X2	576.80
4800	12/14/20X2	127.50
4816	12/15/20X2	80.00
4810	12/16/20X2	50.00
9410	12/21/20X2	621.60

TOTAL CHECKS PAID $ 127,099.14 | C.4.1 |

*All of your recent checks may not be on this statement, either because they haven't cleared yet or they were listed on one of your previous statements.

TRANSACTION DETAIL

Date	Description	Check Number	Withdrawal	Deposit	Ending Balance
12/01/20X2	to Cash: Payroll Account	4784	76,581.10		$324,127.98
12/02/20X2	Daily Bank Deposit			1,728.31	325,856.29
12/03/20X2	Daily Bank Deposit			32,875.55	358,731.84
12/03/20X2	Daily Bank Deposit			27,125.21	385,857.05
12/04/20X2	Daily Bank Deposit			22,771.30	408,628.35
12/05/20X2	Daily Bank Deposit			13,408.80	422,037.15
12/06/20X2	Colorado Dept. of Revenue	4785	1,182.24		420,854.91
12/06/20X2	Mountain Dairy Company	4792	7,491.00		413,363.91
12/07/20X2	Denver City Dept. of Revenue	4786	1,182.23		412,181.68
12/07/20X2	Rocky Mountain Heating and Air Conditioning	4806	444.00		411,737.68
12/07/20X2	Denver Restaurant Supplies	4808	275.00		411,462.68
12/07/20X2	Speedy Fountain Service	4814	456.00		411,006.68
12/08/20X2	Bank of Denver	4791	424.00		410,582.68
12/08/20X2	Cynthia Jamison, Attorney	4805	165.00		410,417.68
12/08/20X2	Summit Cleaners	4807	123.25		410,294.43

	Performed by:
	Reviewed by:

TRANSACTION DETAIL

Date	Description	Check Number	Withdrawal	Deposit	Ending Balance
12/09/20X2	PaperMart	4783	1,466.50		$408,827.93
12/09/20X2	Coastal Farms	4788	7,140.00		401,687.93
12/09/20X2	Colorado Home State Bank	4789	1,745.00		399,942.93
12/09/20X2	Wells Fargo	4790	467.00		399,475.93
12/09/20X2	Boulder Spice Importers	4794	2,657.80		396,818.13
12/09/20X2	State Farm Insurance	4796	345.00		396,473.13
12/09/20X2	Rocky Mountain Property Management	4809	1,584.00		394,889.13
12/09/20X2	Rocky Mountain Kitchen Goods	4815	4,284.00		390,605.13
12/10/20X2	Denver Office Supplies	4793	2,725.00		387,880.13
12/10/20X2	U.S. Post Office	4802	50.40		387,829.73
12/10/20X2	Garcia & Foster CPAs	4803	265.00		387,564.73
12/11/20X2	Milsap Foods	4787	4,565.63		382,999.10
12/11/20X2	Connor Computing	4804	270.00		382,729.10
12/11/20X2	Miguel Lopez	9132	4,990.00		377,739.10
12/12/20X2	Blue Cross/Blue Shield–Colorado	4795	2,700.00		375,039.10
12/12/20X2	Chevron	4811	348.54		374,690.56
12/12/20X2	City of Denver	4813	143.75		374,546.81
12/13/20X2	Farmers Insurance	4798	800.00		373,746.81
12/13/20X2	Farmers Insurance	4799	426.80		373,320.01
12/13/20X2	Verizon	4801	345.00		372,975.01
12/14/20X2	Xcel Energy Company	4797	576.80		372,398.21
12/14/20X2	Qwest Telephone	4800	127.50		372,270.71
12/14/20X2	Daily Bank Deposit			23,013.60	395,284.31
12/15/20X2	Joe's Organic Supplies	4816	80.00		395,204.31
12/16/20X2	Republic Waste Services	4810	50.00		395,154.31
12/19/20X2	Daily Bank Deposit			11,260.80	406,415.11
12/21/20X2	Lindsay McKenna	9410	621.60		405,793.51
12/27/20X2	Daily Bank Deposit			13,161.60	418,955.11
12/27/20X2	Daily Bank Deposit			39,502.86	458,457.97
12/29/20X2	Daily Bank Deposit			211.25	458,669.22
12/31/20X2	Interest			10.00	458,679.22
12/31/20X2	Daily Bank Deposit			5,513.98	464,193.20
12/31/20X2	Bank Service Charge		25.00		464,168.20
12/31/20X2	Check Fees		50.00		$ 464,118.20

Alpine Cupcakes, Inc.
Operating Cash Bank Statement
January 31, 20X3

Bank of Boulder

1573 Market Street
Denver, CO 80202

January 1, 20X3 through January 31, 20X3

Account Number: 5409826

Alpine Cupcakes, Inc.
1250 16th Street
Denver, Colorado 80202

CUSTOMER SERVICE INFORMATION

Service Center:	1-800-555-8342
Hearing Impaired:	1-800-555-3422
Para Española:	1-800-555-1600
International Calls:	1-208-555-1212

CHECKING SUMMARY

	AMOUNT
Beginning Balance	$ 464,118.20
Deposits and Additions	157,210.25
Checks Paid	133,274.88
Bank Charges	25.00
Ending Balance	$ 488,028.57

CHECKS PAID

CHECK NUMBER	DATE PAID	AMOUNT
4817	1/01/20X3	$ 78,496.32
4819	1/03/20X3	1,747.00
4820	1/03/20X3	5,675.76
4824	1/05/20X3	1,745.00
4821	1/06/20X3	1,446.18
4826	1/07/20X3	1.73
4846	1/07/20X3	50.00
4848	1/07/20X3	141.25
4831	1/08/20X3	2,700.00
4832	1/08/20X3	345.00
4835	1/08/20X3	506.00
4836	1/08/20X3	156.00
4843	1/08/20X3	166.75
4847	1/08/20X3	357.96
4849	1/08/20X3	113.75
4818	1/09/20X3	10,376.50
4828	1/09/20X3	8,583.00
4841	1/09/20X3	138.00
4844	1/09/20X3	275.00
4829	1/10/20X3	54.00
4830	1/10/20X3	2,350.00

Performed by:
Reviewed by:

CHECKS PAID (continued)

CHECK NUMBER	DATE PAID	AMOUNT
4822	1/11/20X3	1,446.18
4837	1/11/20X3	318.00
4825	1/12/20X3	467.00
4834	1/12/20X3	800.00
4838	1/12/20X3	51.30
4827	1/13/20X3	3,159.60
4851	1/13/20X3	4,242.00
4842	1/14/20X3	368.00
4845	1/14/20X3	1,584.00
4833	1/15/20X3	593.60
4823	1/15/20X3	4,200.00
4839	1/15/20X3	240.00
4850	1/16/20X3	380.00

TOTAL CHECKS PAID $ 133,274.88

*All of your recent checks may not be on this statement, either because they haven't cleared yet or they were listed on one of your previous statements.

TRANSACTION DETAIL

Date	Description	Check Number	Withdrawal	Deposit	Ending Balance
1/01/20X3	Daily Bank Deposit			37,114.29	$ 501,232.49
1/01/20X3	to Cash: Payroll Account	4817	78,496.32		422,736.17
1/02/20X3	Daily Bank Deposit			5,584.80	428,320.97
1/02/20X3	Daily Bank Deposit			79.77	428,400.74
1/03/20X3	PaperMart	4819	1,747.00		426,653.74
1/03/20X3	Milsap Foods	4820	5,675.76		420,977.98
1/03/20X3	Daily Bank Deposit			26,846.40	447,824.38
1/04/20X3	Daily Bank Deposit			8,200.80	456,025.18
1/05/20X3	Colorado Home State Bank	4824	1,745.00		454,280.18
1/06/20X3	Colorado Dept. of Revenue	4821	1,446.18		452,834.00
1/06/20X3	Daily Bank Deposit			27,139.20	479,973.20
1/07/20X3	Bank of Denver	4826	1.73		479,971.47
1/07/20X3	Republic Waste Services	4846	50.00		479,921.47
1/07/20X3	Jerry's Handiman	4848	141.25		479,780.22
1/07/20X3	Daily Bank Deposit			1,200.00	480,980.22
1/08/20X3	City of Denver	4849	113.75		480,866.47
1/08/20X3	Qwest Telephone	4836	156.00		480,710.47
1/08/20X3	Summit Cleaners	4843	166.75		480,543.72
1/08/20X3	State Farm Insurance	4832	345.00		480,198.72
1/08/20X3	Chevron	4837	357.96		479,840.76

Client Supporting Document

	Performed by:
	Reviewed by:

TRANSACTION DETAIL (continued)

Date	Description	Check Number	Withdrawal	Deposit	Ending Balance
1/08/20X3	Farmers Insurance	4835	506.00		$ 479,334.76
1/08/20X3	Blue Cross/Blue Shield–Colorado	4831	2,700.00		476,634.76
1/09/20X3	Cynthia Jamison, Attorney	4841	138.00		476,496.76
1/09/20X3	Denver Restaurant Supplies	4844	275.00		476,221.76
1/09/20X3	Coastal Farms	4828	8,583.00		467,638.76
1/09/20X3	Mountain Dairy Company	4818	10,376.50		457,262.26
1/10/20X3	Joe's Organic Supplies	4829	54.00		457,208.26
1/10/20X3	Denver Office Supplies	4830	2,350.00		454,858.26
1/11/20X3	Verizon	4837	318.00		454,540.26
1/11/20X3	Denver City Dept. of Revenue	4822	1,446.18		453,094.08
1/12/20X3	U.S. Post Office	4838	51.30		453,042.78
1/12/20X3	Wells Fargo	4825	467.00		452,575.78
1/12/20X3	Farmers Insurance	4834	800.00		451,775.78
1/13/20X3	Boulder Spice Importers	4827	3,159.60		448,616.18
1/13/20X3	Rocky Mountain Kitchen Goods	4851	4,242.00		444,374.18
1/14/20X3	Rocky Mountain Heating and Air Conditioning	4842	368.00		444,006.18
1/14/20X3	Rocky Mountain Property Management	4845	1,584.00		442,422.18
1/14/20X3	Daily Bank Deposit			1,852.80	444,274.98
1/15/20X3	Garcia & Foster CPAs	4839	240.00		444,034.98
1/15/20X3	Xcel Energy Company	4833	593.60		443,441.38
1/15/20X3	Kindle Kitchen Supplies	4823	4,200.00		439,241.38
1/16/20X3	Speedy Fountain Service	4850	380.00		438,861.38
1/26/20X3	Daily Bank Deposit			18,146.34	457,007.72
1/29/20X3	Daily Bank Deposit			2,067.69	459,075.41
1/29/20X3	Daily Bank Deposit			10,648.61	469,724.02
1/31/20X3	Bank Service Fees		25.00		469,699.02
1/31/20X3	Interest			18.00	469,717.02
1/31/20X3	Daily Bank Deposit			18,311.55	$ 488,028.57

Performed by:
ARO 2/8/20X3
Reviewed by:
TES 02/14/20X3

PBC

Date	Check Number	Payee	Outstanding Check Amount	
01/04/20X1	4017	Summit Cleaners	$ 145.00	
03/04/20X1	4077	U.S. Post Office	40.50	
04/04/20X1	4118	Cynthia Jamison, Attorney	153.00	
06/04/20X1	4179	Xcel Energy Company	621.60	
08/04/20X1	4254	Garcia & Foster CPAs	272.50	
09/04/20X1	4279	Joe's Organic Supplies	76.00	
10/04/20X1	4330	Republic Waste Services	50.00	
12/04/20X1	4398	Republic Waste Services	50.00	
01/04/20X2	4437	Speedy Fountain Service	408.00	
03/29/20X2	4508	PaperMart	1,186.00	
04/04/20X2	4539	City of Denver	136.25	
06/04/20X2	4593	Farmers Insurance	404.80	
08/04/20X2	4670	Summit Cleaners	127.60	
09/04/20X2	4698	Qwest Telephone	154.50	
10/31/20X2	4756	Boulder Spice Importers	2,579.40	
11/04/20X2	4777	Republic Waste Services	50.00	
11/28/20X2	4783	PaperMart	1,466.50	Y
11/30/20X2	4784	to Cash: Payroll Account	76,581.10	Y
11/30/20X2	4785	Colorado Dept. of Revenue	1,182.24	Y
11/30/20X2	4786	Denver City Dept. of Revenue	1,182.23	Y
11/30/20X2	4787	Milsap Foods	4,565.63	Y
11/30/20X2	4788	Coastal Farms	7,140.00	Y
		Total O/S Checks November	$ 98,572.85	C.4.1

F

Alpine Cupcakes, Inc.
Operating Deposits in Transit
Nov 30. 20X2

Date	Payee	Amount
11/29/20X2	Daily Bank Deposit	$ 1,728.31
11/30/20X2	Daily Bank Deposit	32,875.55
	Total DIT—Nov.	$ 34,603.86

F

F - Footed.
Y - Traced to clearance on December Bank Statement

Client Supporting Document

C.4.6: pg. 1 of 1

	Performed by:
PBC	*ARO 2/8/20X3* Reviewed by: *TES 02/14/20X3*

Entry No	Date	Sender	Acct. Name	Acct No.	Debit	Credit
1468	12/1/20X2	Mountain Trout Fish House	Cash: Corp.	1101	$15.97	
			A/R	1200		$15.97
1469	12/1/20X2	Southside Café	Cash: Corp.	1101	$20.13	
			A/R	1200		$20.13
1470	12/1/20X2	Country Barrel Restaurants	Cash: Corp.	1101	$6,933.60	
			A/R	1200		$6,933.60
1471	12/1/20X2	Mountain Trout Fish House	Cash: Corp.	1101	$2,299.20	
			A/R	1200		$2,299.20
1472	12/1/20X2	St. Francis Hotel and Spa	Cash: Corp.	1101	$2,047.20	
			A/R	1200		$2,047.20
1473	12/1/20X2	UC Boulder Food Service	Cash: Corp.	1101	$11,455.20	
			A/R	1200		$11,455.20
1474	12/2/20X2	Scotty's Taverns	Cash: Corp.	1101	$10.07	
			A/R	1200		$10.07
1475	12/2/20X2	St. Francis Hotel and Spa	Cash: Corp.	1101	$14.22	
			A/R	1200		$14.22
1476	12/2/20X2	Steinberg Delis	Cash: Corp.	1101	$7.32	
			A/R	1200		$7.32
1477	12/2/20X2	Bon Appetito Restaurants	Cash: Corp.	1101	$10,968.00	
			A/R	1200		$10,968.00
1478	12/2/20X2	Brown's Tavern	Cash: Corp.	1101	$547.20	
			A/R	1200		$547.20
1479	12/2/20X2	High Country Coffee	Cash: Corp.	1101	$4,852.80	
			A/R	1200		$4,852.80
1480	12/2/20X2	Steinberg Delis	Cash: Corp.	1101	$1,053.60	
			A/R	1200		$1,053.60
1481	12/2/20X2	The Sandwich Place	Cash: Corp.	1101	$1,221.60	
			A/R	1200		$1,221.60
1482	12/2/20X2	UC Denver Food Service	Cash: Corp.	1101	$8,450.40	
			A/R	1200		$8,450.40
1483	12/3/20X2	Broken Eggs Restaurant	Cash: Corp.	1101	$1,063.20	
			A/R	1200		$1,063.20
1484	12/3/20X2	Denver Bakery Café	Cash: Corp.	1101	$5,284.80	
			A/R	1200		$5,284.80
1485	12/3/20X2	Granny's Café	Cash: Corp.	1101	$2,620.80	
			A/R	1200		$2,620.80
1486	12/3/20X2	Smokey's Barbeque Pit	Cash: Corp.	1101	$4,440.00	
			A/R	1200		$4,440.00
1487	12/13/20X2	Bon Appetito Restaurants	Cash: Corp.	1101	$15,040.80	
			A/R	1200		$15,040.80

Alpine Cupcakes, Inc.
Cash Receipts Journal—Corporate Account
December 20X2

Performed by:
ARO 2/8/20X3
Reviewed by:
TES 02/14/20X3

Entry No	Date	Sender	Acct. Name	Acct No.	Debit	Credit
1488	12/13/20X2	Elkhorn Coffee Shops	Cash: Corp.	1101	$7,972.80	
			A/R	1200		$7,972.80
1489	12/18/20X2	Bon Appetito Restaurants	Cash: Corp.	1101	$11,260.80	
			A/R	1200		$11,260.80
1490	12/24/20X2	Bon Appetito Restaurants	Cash: Corp.	1101	$13,161.60	
			A/R	1200		$13,161.60
1491	12/25/20X2	Bon Appetito Restaurants	Cash: Corp.	1101	$94.45	
			A/R	1200		$94.45
1492	12/25/20X2	Chavez Cantina	Cash: Corp.	1101	$28.33	
			A/R	1200		$28.33
1493	12/25/20X2	Granny's Café	Cash: Corp.	1101	$22.30	
			A/R	1200		$22.30
1494	12/25/20X2	Mile High Steakhouses	Cash: Corp.	1101	$63.60	
			A/R	1200		$63.60
1495	12/25/20X2	Scotty's Taverns	Cash: Corp.	1101	$2.57	
			A/R	1200		$2.57
1496	12/26/20X2	Broken Eggs Restaurant	Cash: Corp.	1101	$12.18	
			A/R	1200		$12.18
1497	12/26/20X2	Buckhead Restaurants	Cash: Corp.	1101	$27.53	
			A/R	1200		$27.53
1498	12/26/20X2	Julie's Wraps	Cash: Corp.	1101	$16.77	
			A/R	1200		$16.77
1499	12/26/20X2	Luigi's Bistro	Cash: Corp.	1101	$16.53	
			A/R	1200		$16.53
1500	12/26/20X2	Smokey's Barbeque Pit	Cash: Corp.	1101	$29.05	
			A/R	1200		$29.05
1501	12/26/20X2	Bon Appetito Restaurants	Cash: Corp.	1101	$13,600.80	
			A/R	1200		$13,600.80
1502	12/26/20X2	Chavez Cantina	Cash: Corp.	1101	$4,080.00	
			A/R	1200		$4,080.00
1503	12/26/20X2	Country Barrel Restaurants	Cash: Corp.	1101	$7,180.80	
			A/R	1200		$7,180.80
1504	12/26/20X2	High Country Coffee	Cash: Corp.	1101	$6,566.40	
			A/R	1200		$6,566.40
1505	12/26/20X2	Mountain Lion Restaurant	Cash: Corp.	1101	$3,520.80	
			A/R	1200		$3,520.80
1506	12/26/20X2	Papa's Restaurant	Cash: Corp.	1101	$2,611.20	
			A/R	1200		$2,611.20
1507	12/26/20X2	St. Francis Hotel and Spa	Cash: Corp.	1101	$1,840.80	
			A/R	1200		$1,840.80

Alpine Cupcakes, Inc.
Cash Receipts Journal—Corporate Account
December 20X2

Performed by:
ARO 2/8/20X3
Reviewed by:
TES 02/14/20X3

Entry No	Date	Sender	Acct. Name	Acct No.	Debit	Credit
1508	12/27/20X2	Boulder Tea House	Cash: Corp.	1101	$3.33	
			A/R	1200		$3.33
1509	12/27/20X2	Bubba's Fish House	Cash: Corp.	1101	$17.38	
			A/R	1200		$17.38
1510	12/27/20X2	Elkhorn Coffee Shops	Cash: Corp.	1101	$41.43	
			A/R	1200		$41.43
1511	12/27/20X2	Mountain Trout Fish House	Cash: Corp.	1101	$16.15	
			A/R	1200		$16.15
1512	12/27/20X2	Nora's Café	Cash: Corp.	1101	$33.97	
			A/R	1200		$33.97
1513	12/27/20X2	UC Boulder Food Service	Cash: Corp.	1101	$79.65	
			A/R	1200		$79.65
1514	12/27/20X2	UC Denver Food Service	Cash: Corp.	1101	$61.27	
			A/R	1200		$61.27
1515	12/27/20X2	Bubba's Fish House	Cash: Corp.	1101	$2,503.20	
			A/R	1200		$2,503.20
1516	12/27/20X2	Southside Café	Cash: Corp.	1101	$2,757.60	
			A/R	1200		$2,757.60
1517	12/28/20X2	Brown's Tavern	Cash: Corp.	1101	$1.67	
			A/R	1200		$1.67
1518	12/28/20X2	Country Barrel Restaurants	Cash: Corp.	1101	$49.87	
			A/R	1200		$49.87
1519	12/28/20X2	Denver Sirloin Restaurants	Cash: Corp.	1101	$24.55	
			A/R	1200		$24.55
1520	12/28/20X2	Fontana Catering & Café	Cash: Corp.	1101	$16.48	
			A/R	1200		$16.48
1521	12/28/20X2	Little's Grill	Cash: Corp.	1101	$6.53	
			A/R	1200		$6.53
1522	12/28/20X2	Mountain Lion Restaurant	Cash: Corp.	1101	$24.45	
			A/R	1200		$24.45
1523	12/28/20X2	Papa's Restaurant	Cash: Corp.	1101	$18.13	
			A/R	1200		$18.13
1524	12/28/20X2	Pebbles Inn	Cash: Corp.	1101	$3.10	
			A/R	1200		$3.10
1525	12/28/20X2	Southside Café	Cash: Corp.	1101	$19.15	
			A/R	1200		$19.15

Alpine Cupcakes, Inc.
Cash Receipts Journal—Corporate Account
December 20X2

Performed by:
ARO 2/8/20X3
Reviewed by:
TES 02/14/20X3

Entry No	Date	Sender	Acct. Name	Acct No.	Debit	Credit
1526	12/28/20X2	St. Francis Hotel and Spa	Cash: Corp.	1101	$12.78	
			A/R	1200		$12.78
1527	12/28/20X2	Steinberg Delis	Cash: Corp.	1101	$12.18	
			A/R	1200		$12.18
1528	12/28/20X2	The Breakfast Place	Cash: Corp.	1101	$28.75	
			A/R	1200		$28.75
1529	12/28/20X2	The Sandwich Place	Cash: Corp.	1101	$11.05	
			A/R	1200		$11.05
1530	12/28/20X2	Nora's Café	Cash: Corp.	1101	$4,560.00	
			A/R	1200		$4,560.00
1531	12/28/20X2	Mountain Trout Fish House	Cash: Corp.	1101	$2,325.60	
			A/R	1200		$2,325.60
1532	12/28/20X2	Cash: Storefront	Cash: Corp.	1101	$30,000.00	
			Cash: Storefront	1100		$30,000.00
1533	12/29/20X2	Fontana Catering & Café	Cash: Corp.	1101	$2,373.60	
			A/R	1200		$2,373.60
1534	12/29/20X2	Granny's Café	Cash: Corp.	1101	$3,211.20	
			A/R	1200		$3,211.20
1535	12/30/20X2	Julie's Wraps	Cash: Corp.	1101	$2,414.40	
			A/R	1200		$2,414.40
1536	12/30/20X2	The Breakfast Place	Cash: Corp.	1101	$4,140.00	
			A/R	1200		$4,140.00
1537	12/30/20X2	UC Boulder Food Service	Cash: Corp.	1101	$11,469.60	
			A/R	1200		$11,469.60
1538	12/30/20X2	UC Denver Food Service	Cash: Corp.	1101	$8,822.40	
			A/R	1200		$8,822.40
1539	12/31/20X2	Boulder Tea House	Cash: Corp.	1101	$480.00	
			A/R	1200		$480.00
1540	12/31/20X2	Broken Eggs Restaurant	Cash: Corp.	1101	$1,754.40	
			A/R	1200		$1,754.40
1541	12/31/20X2	Elkhorn Coffee Shops	Cash: Corp.	1101	$5,966.40	
			A/R	1200		$5,966.40
Total December 20X2 Cash Receipts					$233,715.69	$233,715.69

PBC

Check Date	Check Number	Check Type	Amount	Payee	Entered in the System	JE Date	
12/1/20X2	4789	payment	$1,745.00	Colorado Home State Bank	yes	12/1/20X2	
12/1/20X2	4790	payment	$467.00	Wells Fargo	yes	12/1/20X2	
12/1/20X2	4791	payment	$424.00	Bank of Denver	yes	12/1/20X2	
12/1/20X2	4792	payment	$7,491.00	Mountain Dairy Company	yes	12/1/20X2	C.2.1
12/3/20X2	4793	payment	$2,725.00	Denver Office Supplies	yes	12/3/20X2	↓
12/4/20X2	4794	payment	$2,657.80	Boulder Spice Importers	yes	12/4/20X2	
12/4/20X2	4795	payment	$2,700.00	Blue Cross/Blue Shield–Colorado	yes	12/4/20X2	
12/4/20X2	4796	payment	$345.00	State Farm Insurance	yes	12/4/20X2	
12/4/20X2	4797	payment	$576.80	Xcel Energy Company	yes	12/4/20X2	
12/4/20X2	4798	payment	$800.00	Farmers Insurance	yes	12/4/20X2	
12/4/20X2	4799	payment	$426.80	Farmers Insurance	yes	12/4/20X2	
12/4/20X2	4800	payment	$127.50	Qwest Telephone	yes	12/4/20X2	
12/4/20X2	4801	payment	$345.00	Verizon	yes	12/4/20X2	
12/4/20X2	4802	payment	$50.40	U.S. Post Office	yes	12/4/20X2	
12/4/20X2	4803	payment	$265.00	Garcia & Foster CPAs	yes	12/4/20X2	
12/4/20X2	4804	payment	$270.00	Connor Computing	yes	12/4/20X2	
12/4/20X2	4805	payment	$165.00	Cynthia Jamison, Attorney	yes	12/4/20X2	C.2.1
12/4/20X2	4806	payment	$444.00	Rocky Mountain Heating and Air Conditioning	yes	12/4/20X2	
12/4/20X2	4807	payment	$123.25	Summit Cleaners	yes	12/4/20X2	
12/4/20X2	4808	payment	$275.00	Denver Restaurant Supplies	yes	12/4/20X2	
12/4/20X2	4809	payment	$1,584.00	Rocky Mountain Property Management	yes	12/4/20X2	
12/4/20X2	4810	payment	$50.00	Republic Waste Services	yes	12/4/20X2	
12/4/20X2	4811	payment	$348.54	Chevron	yes	12/4/20X2	
12/4/20X2	4812	payment	$111.25	Jerry's Handiman	yes	12/4/20X2	
12/4/20X2	4813	payment	$143.75	City of Denver	yes	12/4/20X2	
12/4/20X2	4814	payment	$456.00	Speedy Fountain Service	yes	12/4/20X2	
12/5/20X2	4815	payment	$4,284.00	Rocky Mountain Kitchen Goods	yes	12/5/20X2	C.2.1
12/5/20X2	4816	payment	$80.00	Joe's Organic Supplies	yes	12/5/20X2	
12/28/20X2	4817	payment	$78,496.32	to Cash: Payroll Account	yes	12/28/20X2	C.2.1
12/28/20X2	4818	payment	$10,376.50	Mountain Dairy Company	yes	12/28/20X2	
12/28/20X2	4819	payment	$1,747.00	PaperMart	yes	12/28/20X2	
12/30/20X2	4820	payment	$5,675.76	Milsap Foods	yes	12/30/20X2	C.2.1
12/31/20X2	4821	payment	$1,446.18	Colorado Dept. of Revenue	yes	12/31/20X2	
12/31/20X2	4822	payment	$1,446.18	Denver City Dept. of Revenue	yes	12/31/20X2	
TOTAL DISBURSEMENTS			$128,669.03	C.4.1			

Client Supporting Document

C.4.8: pg. 1 of 1

Garcia and Foster, CPAs

Performed By: *ARO*   **Reviewed By:** *TES*
Date: *2/9/20X3*   **Date:** *02/14/20X3*

Client: Alpine Cupcakes, Inc.
Year End: 12/31/20X2

Per my discussions with Miguel Lopez and Alexis Madison, we found that the client does not have any restricted cash in its bank accounts. In addition, management is not aware of any related party transactions that affected the cash accounts.

Per my review, there are no presentation and disclosure issues related to the cash account.

Alpine Cupcakes, Inc.
Sales and AR Narrative and Walkthrough
Audit Year December 31, 20X2

Garcia and Foster, CPAs

Performed By: *7ES*	**Reviewed By:** SDM
Date: *01/17/20X3*	**Date:** 1/19/20x3

Client: Alpine Cupcakes, Inc.
Year End: 12/31/20X2

The following narrative is updated each year to document our understanding of the client's process and internal controls as they pertain to the sales and accounts receivable processes. To update the narrative for the audit year 20X2, I discussed the processes with Lisa Mercer (corporate sales representative) and Lindsay McKenna (AR manager).

Sales

Sales Transaction Initiated

Sales originate in 2 ways at Alpine Cupcakes. The first is through the storefront, where customers enter and make transactions via cash or charge cards. The second is by sales to businesses, denoted as "corporate" sales. Corporate sales are to businesses that purchase cupcakes from Alpine and then resell them through their restaurants or food service companies.

Sales, Storefront

At the end of 20X2 there were 14 sales associates and 2 store managers, each of whom worked part-time in the storefront. The storefront sells the complete complement of cupcake flavors as well as coffee, milk, hot chocolate, and a variety of sodas. Customers are walk-in and either carry out or sit at one of the café tables to eat their purchases. The storefront accepts MasterCard and VISA. Alpine pays a 3% service fee on credit card transactions. The Company also collects a 4% sales tax for the City of Denver and 4% for the State of Colorado. When customers pay for their purchases, the receipts of these payments go through the cash receipts process. See Document C.1.1. Miguel Lopez makes the cash receipts entries into the accounting records on a daily basis.

Sales, Corporate

Lisa Mercer is the corporate sales representative. She calls each customer monthly to secure a purchase order for the coming month. As Lisa receives the orders from the customers, she creates a sales order. Most of the customers will then fax or email a purchase order to Lisa. If Lisa does not receive a purchase order by the next business day, she will send the customer a copy of the Alpine Sales Order. Corporate sales are all on account. Prior to accepting a new client for credit, Lisa Mercer will review the client's creditworthiness through discussion with the client on the company's ability to pay on a timely basis. As Lisa Mercer prepares each corporate sales order, she will review the customer's creditworthiness based on the company's past history of payments. Lisa makes sure that the customer does not have any payments that are over 90 days past due. Alpine delivers products throughout the month to ensure customers receive fresh baked goods. Lisa stated that she has increased corporate sales for 3 years in a row. In 20X3, Lisa is expecting an increase in her salary since she has consistently increased customer sales.

Garcia and Foster Audit Workpaper

AR.1.1: pg. 1 of 3

Alpine Cupcakes, Inc.
Sales and AR Narrative and Walkthrough
Audit Year December 31, 20X2

Performed By: *7ES*
Date: *01/17/20X3*

Reviewed By: SDM
Date: 1/19/20x3

Sales, Delivery

Alpine's goods are delivered to customers on a weekly basis. The delivery person receives a shipping report from Lisa Mercer and gives the report to the customer upon delivery. The customer then reviews and signs the shipping report and sends the signed report back with the delivery person. The delivery personnel return the signed shipping reports to Lisa Mercer.

Accounts Receivable

AR Process

Lisa Mercer bills each corporate customer at the end of the month for purchases that month that have been delivered. The company recognizes the revenue and related receivable with FOB Destination revenue recognition policy. Lisa also bills shipping costs, of $0.20 per dozen, on a monthly basis at the end of the month. Lisa segregates product and shipping costs into separate bills within the AR account (1200). The invoice includes a due date for customer payments within 30 days of the sales transaction. Lindsay McKenna, AR manager, will review any significant sales transactions on a monthly basis.

Prior to sending each corporate customer an invoice, Lisa ensures that the sales order and corporate purchase order (PO) are complete and without discrepancies. She compares quantities as well as cupcake types with the quantities and types of cupcakes shipped. She also reviews the customer's signatures on the shipping reports. The customers sign upon receipt of the cupcakes to ensure all is in order. When the documentation is complete, Lisa creates an invoice for both product and shipping and sends the bills to the customer. In addition to the sales invoice each month, Alpine provides corporate customers with a Monthly Customer Account Summary which includes current month transactions (new invoices and customer payments) and any past due accounts. If accounts are past due, Lisa will send a second invoice. Miguel Lopez is in charge of sending the monthly customer statements and discussing any discrepancies over the statements with the customers.

Miguel Lopez performs random checks on documents by reconciling the sales order, shipping documents, and sales invoice to validate that all revenue recorded was shipped and that an external PO existed for the transaction. If an external PO does not exist, he will select another transaction to validate. Each department keeps a log of the ordering of document numbers used. Alpine numbers all documents (sales orders, shipping documents, etc.) sequentially. Each employee in charge of creating the documents checks each day to ensure numbers begin each morning with the correct number. Miguel reviews the logs once a month.

Currently, Alpine does not offer a discount for early payment, but the Company is considering a change in this policy.

Uncollectible Accounts

Alpine Cupcakes follows the direct write-off method. Discussions with Lindsay McKenna reveal that account write-offs are very rare (only once in the last 2 years). She credits Lisa Mercer's careful credit checking ability and Lisa's close relationship with each corporate customer for the lack of necessity to

Garcia and Foster Audit Workpaper

AR.1.1: pg. 2 of 3

Performed By: *TES*
Date: *01/17/20X3*

Reviewed By: SDM
Date: 1/19/20x3

Uncollectible Accounts (continued)

write off accounts. She does reveal that Alpine will work with customers who have temporary difficulties with payments, and that the Company will continue to sell products to such customers as long as they are making payments on past due amounts.

Sales Returns and Allowances

Alpine has policies in place to ensure customer satisfaction with all goods. First, customers inspect goods upon delivery and sign for the goods with the delivery person, attesting to the condition of the goods upon delivery. Second, if a customer rejects a product, the delivery person calls Lisa Mercer, and Lisa arranges for substitute cupcakes to be delivered within 24 hours. Second, customers must return goods not rejected at receiving within 24 hours. Lisa creates a credit memorandum and credits the customer's AR account for the returned goods at sales price.   Lindsay McKenna (AR manager) reviews all credit memorandums.

Lisa Mercer is responsible for creating a quarterly estimate of sales returns and allowance. Because of the 24-hour return policy and the Alpine policy requiring customers to inspect goods upon delivery, the estimate for returns and allowances has always been immaterial.

Walkthrough Procedures: I performed a walkthrough of the sales and accounts receivable transactions. The storefront sales transactions are part of the cash portion of the audit, so I walked through the corporate sales transactions and AR transactions with Lisa Mercer. Since she had already contacted the customers for their monthly sales orders, Lisa described the process to me and showed me the documents for the February sales order for Mountain Dairy. Lisa also described the billing process and walked through an example of how she would create a sales invoice. She will perform the billing process for February at the end of the month. Per discussion with Lindsay McKenna, she has not had to review any sales transactions in 20X2 as Lisa has been doing a great job of the billing process. Per her review of the monthly sales, all customer sales totals appeared to be normal. Per discussion with Miguel Lopez, he performed a random check of the documents and the log sheets in March 20X2 and in August 20X2. He walked me through the documents that he reviews. The processes appear to follow the description provided in the narrative. No exceptions were noted in the walkthrough.

Alpine Cupcakes, Inc.
Corporate Sales and AR Flowchart
Audit Year December 31, 20X2

Garcia and Foster, CPAs

Performed By: *TES*   **Reviewed By:** SDM
Date: *01/17/20X3*   **Date:** 1/19/20x3

Corporate Sales and AR Flowchart:

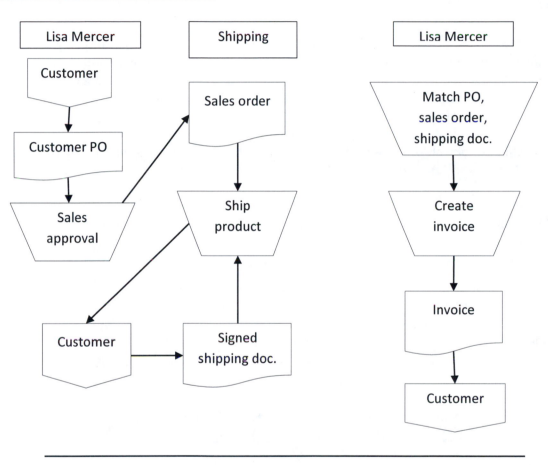

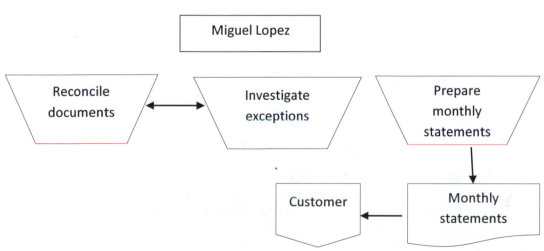

Alpine Cupcakes, Inc.
AR TOC Memo
Audit Year December 31, 20X2

Garcia and Foster, CPAs

Performed By: *TES*
Date: *01/23/20X3*

Reviewed By: SDM
Date: 1/29/20x3

Client: Alpine Cupcakes, Inc.
Year End: 12/31/20X2

The company compares the customer purchase order, approved sales order, and shipping documents prior to creating the sales invoice and booking the sales transaction. The company's controls require them to obtain these documents prior to making a sales entry. As part of the control, Lisa Mercer will compare the quantity and prices on all of the documents. If there are any discrepancies between the documents, Lisa Mercer will investigate prior to booking the entry.

As part of our testing of controls procedures, we reperformed the company's internal control over the sales process. We used attribute sampling to select a sample from the sales journal and evaluate the results.

1. Test Objective: *To determine if the client's controls over the sales process are sufficient to prevent and detect errors.*
2. Population: *All sales recorded in the sales journal.*
3. Sampling unit: *An individual invoice recorded in the sales journal.*
4. Risk of assessing control risk too low: *10%*
5. Tolerable deviation rate: *6%*
6. Expected population deviation rate: *2%*
7. Sample size (from table below): *88 individual sales, with 2 allowable deviations*
8. Deviation: *When the quantities and/or prices do not agree between the customer purchase order, approved sales order, invoice, and shipping documents.*

Determination of Sample Size: Risk of Assessing Control Risk Too Low 10%
(Allowable number of deviations in parentheses)

Expected Deviation Rate	Tolerable Rate 4%		5%		6%		7%		8%	
0.0%	57	(0)	45	(0)	38	(0)	32	(0)	28	(0)
0.5%	96	(1)	77	(1)	64	(1)	55	(1)	48	(1)
1.0%	96	(1)	77	(1)	64	(1)	55	(1)	48	(1)
1.5%	132	(2)	105	(2)	64	(1)	55	(1)	48	(1)
2.0%	198	(4)	132	(3)	88	(2)	75	(2)	48	(1)
3.0%	*		*		132	(4)	94	(3)	65	(2)

* Sample size is too large to be cost-effective for most audit applications.
Source: AICPA Audit Guide, *Audit Sampling* (New York, 2014).

Using a random number generator, we selected 88 transactions from the sales journal and requested the supporting documentation to reperform the client's internal controls. We requested the documents on February 1st and Lisa Mercer provided us with the documents on February 6th.

Garcia and Foster Audit Workpaper

AR.2.1 pg. 1 of 2

Performed By: *TES*   **Reviewed By:** SDM
Date: *01/23/20X3*   **Date:** 1/29/20x3

Determination of Sample Size (continued):
During our reperformance of the client's control procedures, we found no deviations in the documentation.

Evaluation of Results:
9. Actual number of deviations found: *0*
10. Sample size: *88*
11. Achieved upper precision limit (from table below): *Because sample size is 88 (not in the table), we use the closest sample size in the table (90). Sample size of 90 with 0 deviations = AUPL of 2.6%.*
12. Compare AUPL to tolerable deviation rate:

    AUPL of 2.6%   <   Tolerable deviation rate of 6%

13. Final conclusion: *Because the achieved upper precision limit is less than the tolerable deviation rate, we conclude that the client's control procedures over the sales process are operating effectively.*

Evaluation of Results: Risk of Assessing Control Risk Too Low 10%

Sample Size	Actual number of deviations found				
	0	**1**	**2**	**3**	**4**
30	7.4	12.4	16.8	*	*
40	5.6	9.4	12.8	16	19
50	4.6	7.6	10.3	12.9	15.4
60	3.8	6.4	8.7	10.8	12.9
70	3.3	5.5	7.5	9.3	11.1
80	2.9	4.8	6.6	8.2	9.8
90	2.6	4.3	5.9	7.3	8.7
100	2.3	3.9	5.3	6.6	7.9

* Over 20%.
Source: AICPA Audit Guide, *Audit Sampling* (New York, 2014).

Performed by:
TES 01/23/20X3
Reviewed by:
SDM 1/29/20x3

		ALPINE CUPCAKES SALES JOURNAL: SAMPLE SELECTED		
Sample Observation	Date	Customer Name	Total Sales	*Note*
1	1/1/X2	Buckhead Restaurants	$1,207.20	√
2	1/10/X2	Pebbles Inn	$554.40	√
3	1/11/X2	Bubba's Fish House	$2,049.60	√
4	1/14/X2	Luigi's Bistro	$640.80	√
5	1/15/X2	Boulder Tea House	$314.40	√
6	1/15/X2	Fontana Catering & Café	$2,205.60	√
7	1/15/X2	Granny's Café	$3,120.00	√
8	1/16/X2	Bon Appetito Restaurants	$9,717.60	√
9	1/17/X2	Denver Bakery Café	$5,004.00	√
10	1/17/X2	Julie's Wraps	$2,220.00	√
11	1/23/X2	Papa's Restaurant	$2,822.40	√
12	2/1/X2	High Country Coffee	$5,378.40	*Note 1*
13	2/3/X2	Nora's Café	$4,884.00	√
14	2/7/X2	Boulder Tea House	$1,831.20	√
15	2/8/X2	Buckhead Restaurants	$3,400.80	√
16	2/13/X2	Chavez Cantina	$3,842.40	√
17	2/16/X2	Mountain Lion Restaurant	$2,035.20	√
18	2/17/X2	Bon Appetito Restaurants	$13,219.20	√
19	2/17/X2	Broken Eggs Restaurant	$1,761.60	√
20	2/18/X2	The Breakfast Place	$5,121.60	√
21	2/28/X2	Steinberg Delis	$4,012.80	√
22	3/1/X2	Country Barrel Restaurants	$6,220.80	√
23	3/3/X2	Julie's Wraps	$2,092.80	√
24	3/4/X2	Mountain Lion Restaurant	$2,323.20	√
25	3/9/X2	Granny's Café	$1,024.80	√
26	3/9/X2	Little's Grill	$1,396.80	
27	3/10/X2	The Breakfast Place	$2,728.80	√
28	3/11/X2	Smokey's Barbeque Pit	$2,661.60	√
29	3/24/X2	Papa's Restaurant	$1,372.80	√
30	3/28/X2	The Sandwich Place	$530.40	√
31	4/7/X2	Nora's Café	$2,565.60	√
32	4/11/X2	Bon Appetito Restaurants	$10,536.00	√
33	4/11/X2	Steinberg Delis	$2,839.20	√
34	4/12/X2	Chavez Cantina	$2,995.20	√
35	4/12/X2	Country Barrel Restaurants	$4,665.60	√
36	4/19/X2	Broken Eggs Restaurant	$405.60	√
37	4/21/X2	Mountain Lion Restaurant	$1,228.80	√
38	4/23/X2	Granny's Café	$1,504.80	√

Garcia and Foster Audit Workpaper

AR.2.2 pg. 1 of 3

Alpine Cupcakes, Inc.
20X2 Sales Journal Excerpt
Audit Year December 31, 20X2

ALPINE CUPCAKES SALES JOURNAL: SAMPLE SELECTED

Sample Observation	Date	Customer Name	Total Sales	Note
39	4/25/X2	Boulder Tea House	$854.40	√
40	4/26/X2	St. Francis Hotel and Spa	$1,836.00	√
41	5/5/X2	Steinberg Delis	$1,012.80	√
42	5/7/X2	Southside Café	$1,485.60	√
43	5/7/X2	UC Boulder Food Service	$7,656.00	√
44	5/8/X2	Boulder Tea House	$1,204.80	√
45	5/8/X2	Papa's Restaurant	$2,709.60	√
46	5/9/X2	Mountain Lion Restaurant	$1,684.80	√
47	5/10/X2	Buckhead Restaurants	$1,555.20	√
48	5/25/X2	Bubba's Fish House	$2,088.00	√
49	6/17/X2	High Country Coffee	$6,969.60	√
50	6/19/X2	Denver Bakery Café	$5,006.40	√
51	6/27/X2	Pebbles Inn	$398.40	√
52	7/10/X2	Bubba's Fish House	$3,060.00	√
53	7/11/X2	Mile High Steakhouses	$9,369.60	√
54	7/12/X2	Mountain Trout Fish House	$2,092.80	√
55	7/13/X2	Granny's Café	$2,292.00	√
56	7/22/X2	Boulder Tea house	$1,173.60	Note 1 →
57	7/23/X2	UC Denver Food Service	$10,704.00	√
58	7/24/X2	Julie's Wraps	$2,743.20	√
59	7/26/X2	The Breakfast Place	$5,349.60	√
60	8/4/X2	Scotty's Taverns	$2,812.80	√
61	8/6/X2	Steinberg Delis	$1,869.60	√
62	8/11/X2	Bon Appetito Restaurants	$15,040.80	
63	8/15/X2	The Breakfast Place	$4,886.40	√
64	8/16/X2	Boulder Tea House	$432.00	√
65	9/3/X2	Boulder Tea House	$285.60	√
66	9/16/X2	Luigi's Bistro	$2,224.80	√
67	9/16/X2	Nora's Café	$3,475.20	√
68	9/17/X2	Buckhead Restaurants	$1,852.80	√
69	9/22/X2	Southside Café	$960.00	
70	9/26/X2	Little's Grill	$1,034.40	√
71	10/1/X2	Nora's Café	$4,560.00	√
72	10/1/X2	The Sandwich Place	$1,221.60	√
73	10/9/X2	Mile High Steakhouses	$10,108.80	√
74	10/14/X2	Papa's Restaurant	$3,580.80	√
75	10/20/X2	Granny's Café	$2,620.80	√

Performed by:
TES 01/23/20X3
Reviewed by:
SDM 1/29/20X3

ALPINE CUPCAKES SALES JOURNAL: SAMPLE SELECTED				
Sample Observation	Date	Customer Name	Total Sales	Note
76	11/1/X2	Broken Eggs Restaurant	$1,754.40	√
77	11/4/X2	Buckhead Restaurants	$3,964.80	√
78	11/4/X2	Julie's Wraps	$2,414.40	√
79	11/6/X2	Scotty's Taverns	$369.60	√
80	11/8/X2	Little's Grill	$940.80	√
81	11/11/X2	The Sandwich Place	$1,591.20	√
82	11/18/X2	High Country Coffee	$6,566.40	√
83	11/27/X2	The Breakfast Place	$4,140.00	√
84	12/2/X2	The Breakfast Place	$4,116.00	√
85	12/5/X2	Buckhead Restaurants	$2,642.40	√
86	12/13/X2	Denver Bakery Café	$5,791.20	√
87	12/23/X2	Bon Appetito Restaurants	$16,968.00	√
88	12/27/X2	Country Barrel Restaurants	$8,452.80	√
		Total Sales in Sample	$310,360.80	
		Total Product Sales	$1,455,381.60	
		Percent Coverage	21%	
		Shipping Revenue	$10,106.82	
		Total Corporate Revenue	$1,465,488.42	

√ For random sample of 88 sales from sales journal, we obtained customer purchase order, sales order, and shipping documents. We reperformed the client control over sales and accounts receivable and agreed quantities and prices between all documents and amounts recorded in sales journal.

Note 1: For High Country Coffee invoice dated 2/28/20X2, and Boulder Tea House invoice dated 7/31/20X2, Alpine omitted printing the Vanilla Cupcakes on the invoice. The correct quantities were shipped to the customer and the customer was billed and paid the correct dollar amount. According to Miguel Lopez, they had a "snafu" in the invoicing software that caused it to omit printing the Vanilla Cupcakes, but bill the correct dollar amounts. Miguel says the "snafu" has been fixed. See documentation on AR.2.3 and AR.2.4.

Because the correct quantities were shipped to the customer and the customer was billed and paid the correct dollar amount, these are not counted as deviations in our test of controls.

Performed by:
TES 01/23/20X3
Reviewed by:
SDM 1/29/20x3

PURCHASE ORDER

Boulder Tea House
1700 13th Street
Boulder, Colorado 80302

Purchased From:	**Purchase order:** 1015
Alpine Cupcakes, Inc.	**Date:** 7/2/20X2
1250 16th Street	**Page** 1
Denver, CO 80202	

Ordered		Unit	Description	Tax	Unit Price		Total
49	√	cupcake	Carrot Cake		$2.40	μ	$117.60
93		cupcake	Chocolate		$2.40		$223.20
29		cupcake	Gluten-free Chocolate		$2.40		$69.60
64		cupcake	Lemon		$2.40		$153.60
34		cupcake	Red Velvet		$2.40		$81.60
34		cupcake	Spice		$2.40		$81.60
172		cupcake	Vanilla		$2.40		$412.80
14		cupcake	Almond Vegan		$2.40		$33.60

Purchase Approved By: *Jenny Jenkins*

Purchase Approval Date: _7/2/20x2_

Total
Amount $1,173.60

PMT Received
8/29/20X2

Lindsay McKenna

Alpine Shipping slip Numbers: **26030, 26141, 26182, 26203, 26221, 26269, 26288, 26351**

Alpine Invoice Number: **6273**

Tickmark Legend:

√ - *tied quantity between documents*

μ - *tied price between documents*

Performed by:
TES 01/23/20X3
Reviewed by:
SDM 1/29/20x3

SALES ORDER

Alpine Cupcakes, Inc.
1250 16th Street
Denver, Colorado 80202

Sales to:	Boulder Tea House		Order No.:	2596
Address	1700 13th Street		Call Date:	7/1/20X2
	Boulder, CO 80302		Page	1

Ordered		Unit	Description	Tax	Unit Price		Total
49	√	Cupcake	Carrot Cake		$2.40	μ	$117.60
93		Cupcake	Chocolate		$2.40		$223.20
29		Cupcake	Gluten-free Chocolate		$2.40		$69.60
64		Cupcake	Lemon		$2.40		$153.60
34		Cupcake	Red Velvet		$2.40		$81.60
34		Cupcake	Spice		$2.40		$81.60
172		Cupcake	Vanilla		$2.40		$412.80
14		Cupcake	Almond Vegan		$2.40		$33.60

Sale Made By: *Lisa Mercer*

Sale Date: __7/1/20X2__

Total

Amount $1,173.60

PMT Received 8/29/20X2

Lindsay McKenna

Customer PO Number: *1015*

Alpine Shipping slip Numbers: *26030, 26141, 26182, 26203, 26221, 26269, 26288, 26351*

Alpine Invoice Number: *6273*

Tickmark Legend:

√ – *tied quantity between documents*

μ – *tied price between documents*

Performed by:
TES 01/23/20X3
Reviewed by:
SDM 1/29/20x3

PRODUCT INVOICE

Alpine Cupcakes, Inc.
1250 16th Street
Denver, Colorado 80202

Page 1/4

Shipped To:

Boulder Tea House
1700 13th Street
Boulder, CO 80302

Customer PO: 1015
Customer PO Date: 7/02/20X2

Invoice Number: 6273
Date: 7/31/20X2
Due Date: 8/31/20X2
Sales Order No: 2596

No. Ordered	Date Shipped	Number Shipped	No. left in order	Description	Price	Total
49	7/5/20X2	6 √	43	Carrot Cake	$2.40 μ	$14.40
93	7/5/20X2	12	81	Chocolate	$2.40	$28.80
29	7/5/20X2	4	25	Gluten-free Choc.	$2.40	$9.60
64	7/5/20X2	8	56	Lemon	$2.40	$19.20
34	7/5/20X2	4	30	Red Velvet	$2.40	$9.60
34	7/5/20X2	4	30	Spice	$2.40	$9.60
172	7/5/20X2	22	150	Vanilla	$2.40	$52.80
14	7/5/20X2	2	12	Almond Vegan	$2.40	$4.80
				Shipment Total		**$148.80**
49	7/8/20X2	6	37	Carrot Cake	$2.40	$14.40
93	7/8/20X3	12	69	Chocolate	$2.40	$28.80
29	7/8/20X4	4	21	Gluten-free Choc.	$2.40	$9.60
64	7/8/20X5	8	48	Lemon	$2.40	$19.20
34	7/8/20X6	4	26	Red Velvet	$2.40	$9.60
34	7/8/20X7	4	26	Spice	$2.40	$9.60
172	7/8/20X8	22	128	Vanilla	$2.40	$52.80
14	7/8/20X9	2	10	Almond Vegan	$2.40	$4.80
				Shipment Total		**$148.80**
49	7/12/20X2	6	31	Carrot Cake	$2.40	$14.40
93	7/12/20X2	12	57	Chocolate	$2.40	$28.80
29	7/12/20X2	4	17	Gluten-free Choc.	$2.40	$9.60
64	7/12/20X2	8	40	Lemon	$2.40	$19.20
34	7/12/20X2	4	22	Red Velvet	$2.40	$9.60
34	7/12/20X2	4	22	Spice	$2.40	$9.60
172	7/12/20X2	22	106	Vanilla	$2.40	$52.80
14	7/12/20X2	2	8	Almond Vegan	$2.40	$4.80
				Shipment Total		**$148.80**

Performed by:
TES 01/23/20X3
Reviewed by:
SDM 1/29/20x3

PRODUCT INVOICE (continued)

Alpine Cupcakes, Inc.
1250 16th Street
Denver, Colorado 80202

Page 2/4

Shipped To:

Invoice Number: 6273

Boulder Tea House

Date: 7/31/20X2

1700 13th Street

Boulder, CO 80302

Ordered	Date Shipped	Number Shipped	No. left in order	Description	Price	Total
49	7/15/20X2	6 √	25	Carrot Cake	$2.40 μ	$14.40
93	7/15/20X2	12	45	Chocolate	$2.40	$28.80
29	7/15/20X2	4	13	Gluten-free Choc.	$2.40	$9.60
64	7/15/20X2	8	32	Lemon	$2.40	$19.20
34	7/15/20X2	4	18	Red Velvet	$2.40	$9.60
34	7/15/20X2	4	18	Spice	$2.40	$9.60
172	7/15/20X2	22	84	Vanilla	$2.40	$52.80
14	7/15/20X2	2	6	Almond Vegan	$2.40	$4.80
				Shipment Total		**$148.80**
49	7/19/20X2	6	19	Carrot Cake	$2.40	$14.40
93	7/19/20X2	12	33	Chocolate	$2.40	$28.80
29	7/19/20X2	4	9	Gluten-free Choc.	$2.40	$9.60
64	7/19/20X2	8	24	Lemon	$2.40	$19.20
34	7/19/20X2	4	14	Red Velvet	$2.40	$9.60
34	7/19/20X2	4	14	Spice	$2.40	$9.60
172	7/19/20X2	22	62	Vanilla	$2.40	$52.80
14	7/19/20X2	2	4	Almond Vegan	$2.40	$4.80
				Shipment Total		**$148.80**
49	7/24/20X2	6	13	Carrot Cake	$2.40	$14.40
93	7/24/20X2	12	21	Chocolate	$2.40	$28.80
29	7/24/20X2	4	5	Gluten-free Choc.	$2.40	$9.60
64	7/24/20X2	8	16	Lemon	$2.40	$19.20
34	7/24/20X2	4	10	Red Velvet	$2.40	$9.60
34	7/24/20X2	4	10	Spice	$2.40	$9.60
172	7/24/20X2	22	40	Vanilla	$2.40	$52.80
14	7/24/20X2	2	2	Almond Vegan	$2.40	$4.80
				Shipment Total		**$148.80**

Performed by:
TES 01/23/20X3
Reviewed by:
SDM 1/29/20X3

PRODUCT INVOICE (continued)

Alpine Cupcakes, Inc.
1250 16th Street
Denver, Colorado 80202

Page 3/4

Shipped To:

Boulder Tea House

1700 13th Street

Boulder, CO 80302

Invoice Number: 6273

Date: 7/31/20X2

Ordered	Date Shipped	Number Shipped		No. left in order	Description	Price		Total
49	7/27/20X2	6	√	7	Carrot Cake	$2.40	μ	$14.40
93	7/27/20X2	12		9	Chocolate	$2.40		$28.80
29	7/27/20X2	4		1	Gluten-free Choc.	$2.40		$9.60
64	7/27/20X2	8		8	Lemon	$2.40		$19.20
34	7/27/20X2	4		6	Red Velvet	$2.40		$9.60
34	7/27/20X2	4		6	Spice	$2.40		$9.60
172	7/27/20X2	22		18	Vanilla	$2.40		$52.80
14	7/27/20X2	2		0	Almond Vegan	$2.40		$4.80
					Shipment Total			**$148.80**
49	7/31/20X2	7		0	Carrot Cake	$2.40		$16.80
93	7/31/20X2	9		0	Chocolate	$2.40		$21.60
29	7/31/20X2	1		0	Gluten-free Choc.	$2.40		$2.40
64	7/31/20X2	8		0	Lemon	$2.40		$19.20
34	7/31/20X2	6		0	Red Velvet	$2.40		$14.40
34	7/31/20X2	6		0	Spice	$2.40		$14.40
14	7/31/20X2	0		0	Almond Vegan	$2.40		$0.00
					Shipment Total			**$132.00**

See Note A

Sales Tax	N/A
Freight	N/A
Invoice Total	$1,173.60

Tickmark Legend: √ - tied quantity between documents   μ - tied price between documents

Note A: For the last shipment of the month, the Vanilla cupcakes did not print on the invoice. The correct quantities were shipped to the customer and the customer was billed and paid the correct dollar amount. According to Miguel Lopez, they had a "snafu" in the invoicing software that caused it to omit printing the Vanilla cupcakes on the invoice. Miguel says the "snafu" has been fixed. Because the customer was shipped and billed correctly in total, this is not an exception. See Note 1 at AR 2.2.

Performed by:
TES 01/23/20X3
Reviewed by:
SDM 1/29/20x3

PRODUCT INVOICE

Remittance Advice

Boulder Tea House
1700 13th Street
Boulder, CO 80302

Page 4/4

Invoice Number:	6273
Sales Order No:	2596
Customer PO:	1015
Customer PO Date:	7/02/20X2
Amount Due:	$1,173.60
Date Due:	8/30/20X2

Date Paid   _____

Amount Paid   _____

Pmt Received
8/29/20X2

Lindsay McKenna

See returned remittance form

Performed by:
TES 01/23/20X3
Reviewed by:
SDM 1/29/20x3

ALPINE CUPCAKES, INC.
Shipping Report

Date: 7/5/20X2
Purchase Order #: 1015
Shipped To: Boulder Tea House
Freight Carrier: Alpine Cupcake Carrier

Shipping Report # 26030

Quantity		Unit	Description
6	√	Cupcakes	Carrot Cake
12		Cupcakes	Chocolate
4		Cupcakes	Gluten-free Chocolate
8		Cupcakes	Lemon
4		Cupcakes	Red Velvet
4		Cupcakes	Spice
22		Cupcakes	Vanilla
2		Cupcakes	Almond Vegan

Remarks: Items received in OK condition
Received By: Karen Tompson
Delivered To: Receiving Dept.

ALPINE CUPCAKES, INC.
Shipping Report

Date: 7/8/20X2
Purchase Order #: 1015
Shipped To: Boulder Tea House
Freight Carrier: Alpine Cupcake Carrier

Shipping Report # 26141

Quantity		Unit	Description
6	√	Cupcakes	Carrot Cake
12		Cupcakes	Chocolate
4		Cupcakes	Gluten-free Chocolate
8		Cupcakes	Lemon
4		Cupcakes	Red Velvet
4		Cupcakes	Spice
22		Cupcakes	Vanilla
2		Cupcakes	Almond Vegan

Remarks: Items received in OK condition
Received By: Karen Tompson
Delivered To: Receiving Dept.

Performed by:
TES 01/23/20X3
Reviewed by:
SDM 1/29/20x3

ALPINE CUPCAKES, INC.
Shipping Report

Date: 7/12/20X2

Purchase Order #: 1015

Shipped To: Boulder Tea House

Freight Carrier: Alpine Cupcake Carrier

Shipping Report # 26182

Quantity		Unit	Description
6	√	Cupcakes	Carrot Cake
12		Cupcakes	Chocolate
4		Cupcakes	Gluten-free Chocolate
8		Cupcakes	Lemon
4		Cupcakes	Red Velvet
4		Cupcakes	Spice
22		Cupcakes	Vanilla
2		Cupcakes	Almond Vegan

Remarks: *Items received in OK condition*

Received By: *Karen Tompson*

Delivered To: *Receiving Dept.*

ALPINE CUPCAKES, INC.
Shipping Report

Date: 7/15/20X2

Purchase Order #: 1015

Shipped To: Boulder Tea House

Freight Carrier: Alpine Cupcake Carrier

Shipping Report # 26203

Quantity		Unit	Description
6	√	Cupcakes	Carrot Cake
12		Cupcakes	Chocolate
4		Cupcakes	Gluten-free Chocolate
8		Cupcakes	Lemon
4		Cupcakes	Red Velvet
4		Cupcakes	Spice
22		Cupcakes	Vanilla
2		Cupcakes	Almond Vegan

Remarks: *Items received in OK condition*

Received By: *Karen Tompson*

Delivered To: *Receiving Dept.*

Client Supporting Document

AR.2.3: pg. 8 of 11

Performed by:
TES 01/23/20X3
Reviewed by:
SDM 1/29/20x3

ALPINE CUPCAKES, INC.
Shipping Report

Date:	7/19/20X2	
Purchase Order #:	1015	**Shipping Report # 26221**
Shipped To:	Boulder Tea House	
Freight Carrier:	Alpine Cupcake Carrier	

Quantity	Unit	Description
6	Cupcakes	Carrot Cake
12	Cupcakes	Chocolate
4	Cupcakes	Gluten-free Chocolate
8	Cupcakes	Lemon
4	Cupcakes	Red Velvet
4	Cupcakes	Spice
22	Cupcakes	Vanilla
2	Cupcakes	Almond Vegan

Remarks: _Items received in OK condition_

Received By: _Karen Tompson_

Delivered To: _Receiving Dept._

ALPINE CUPCAKES, INC.
Shipping Report

Date:	7/24/20X2	
Purchase Order #:	1015	**Shipping Report # 26269**
Shipped To:	Boulder Tea House	
Freight Carrier:	Alpine Cupcake Carrier	

Quantity	Unit	Description
6	Cupcakes	Carrot Cake
12	Cupcakes	Chocolate
4	Cupcakes	Gluten-free Chocolate
8	Cupcakes	Lemon
4	Cupcakes	Red Velvet
4	Cupcakes	Spice
22	Cupcakes	Vanilla
2	Cupcakes	Almond Vegan

Remarks: _Items received in OK condition_

Received By: _Karen Tompson_

Delivered To: _Receiving Dept._

Performed by:
TES 01/23/20X3
Reviewed by:
SDM 1/29/20x3

ALPINE CUPCAKES, INC.
Shipping Report

Date: 7/27/20X2

Purchase Order #: 1015   **Shipping Report # 26288**

Shipped To: Boulder Tea House

Freight Carrier: Alpine Cupcake Carrier

Quantity		Unit	Description
6	√	Cupcakes	Carrot Cake
12		Cupcakes	Chocolate
4		Cupcakes	Gluten-free Chocolate
8		Cupcakes	Lemon
4		Cupcakes	Red Velvet
4		Cupcakes	Spice
22		Cupcakes	Vanilla
2		Cupcakes	Almond Vegan

Remarks: _Items received in OK condition_

Received By: _Karen Tompson_

Delivered To: _Receiving Dept._

ALPINE CUPCAKES, INC.
Shipping Report

Date: 7/31/20X2

Purchase Order #: 1015   **Shipping Report # 26351**

Shipped To: Boulder Tea House

Freight Carrier: Alpine Cupcake Carrier

Quantity		Unit	Description
7	√	Cupcakes	Carrot Cake
9		Cupcakes	Chocolate
1		Cupcakes	Gluten-free Chocolate
8		Cupcakes	Lemon
6		Cupcakes	Red Velvet
6		Cupcakes	Spice
18		Cupcakes	Vanilla
0		Cupcakes	Almond Vegan

Remarks: _Items received in OK condition_

Received By: _Karen Tompson_

Delivered To: _Receiving Dept._

Tickmark Legend: √ - *tied quantity between documents* μ - *tied price between documents*

Performed by:
TES 01/23/20X3
Reviewed by:
SDM 1/29/20x3

Please return this page with your payment

PRODUCT INVOICE

Remittance Advice

Page 4/4

Boulder Tea House	Invoice Number: 6273
1700 13th Street	Sales Order No: 2596
Boulder, CO 80302	Customer PO: 1015
	Customer PO Date: 7/02/20X2
	Amount Due: $1,173.60

Date Paid	8/29/20X2	
Amount Paid	$1,173.60	μ

**PMT RECEIVED
8/29/20X2**

Tickmark Legend:
√ – *tied quantity between documents*
μ – *tied price between documents*

Lindsay McKenna

Performed by:
TES 01/23/20X3
Reviewed by:
SDM 1/29/20x3

PURCHASE ORDER

High Country Coffee
3900 @ 32nd Street
Denver, CO 80212

Purchased From:
Alpine Cupcakes, Inc.
1250 16th Street
Denver, CO 80202

Purchase order:	7915
Date:	2/1/20X2
Page	1

Ordered	Unit	Description	Tax	Unit Price	Total
224 √	cupcake	Carrot Cake		$2.40 μ	$537.60 √
426	cupcake	Chocolate		$2.40	$1,022.40
134	cupcake	Gluten-free Chocolate		$2.40	$321.60
291	cupcake	Lemon		$2.40	$698.40
157	cupcake	Red Velvet		$2.40	$376.80
157	cupcake	Spice		$2.40	$376.80
785	cupcake	Vanilla		$2.40	$1,884.00
67	cupcake	Almond Vegan		$2.40	$160.80

Purchase Approved By: *Thomas Brown*

Purchase Approval Date: _2/1/20x2_

Total	
Amount	$5,378.40

**PMT Received
3/30/20X2**

Lindsay McKenna
Alpine Shipping slip Numbers: **24370, 24402, 24456, 24523, 24578, 24598, 24624, 24681**
Alpine Invoice Number: **6120**

Tickmark Legend:
√ – *tied quantity between documents*
μ – *tied price between documents*

Performed by:
TES 01/23/20X3
Reviewed by:
SDM 1/29/20x3

SALES ORDER

Alpine Cupcakes, Inc.
1250 16th Street
Denver, Colorado 80202

Sales to:	High Country Coffee	Order No.:	2443
Address	3900 @ 32nd Street	Call Date:	2/1/20X2
	Denver, CO 80212	Page	1

Ordered	Unit	Description	Tax	Unit Price	Total
224 √	cupcake	Carrot Cake		$2.40 μ	$537.60 √
426	cupcake	Chocolate		$2.40	$1,022.40
134	cupcake	Gluten-free Chocolate		$2.40	$321.60
291	cupcake	Lemon		$2.40	$698.40
157	cupcake	Red Velvet		$2.40	$376.80
157	cupcake	Spice		$2.40	$376.80
785	cupcake	Vanilla		$2.40	$1,884.00
67	cupcake	Almond Vegan		$2.40	$160.80

Sale Made By: *Lisa Mercer*

Sale Date: __7/1/20X2__

Total

Amount $5,378.40

PMT Received
3/30/20X2

Lindsay McKenna

Customer PO Number: 7915
Alpine Shipping slip Numbers: *24370, 24402, 24456, 24523, 24578, 24598, 24624, 24681*
Alpine Invoice Number: *6120*

Tickmark Legend:
√ - *tied quantity between documents*
μ - *tied price between documents*

Performed by:
TES 01/23/20X3
Reviewed by:
SDM 1/29/20x3

PRODUCT INVOICE

Alpine Cupcakes, Inc.
1250 16th Street
Denver, Colorado 80202

Page 1/4

Shipped To:

High Country Coffee
3900 @ 32nd Street
Denver, CO 80212

Customer PO: 7915
Customer PO Date: 2/1/20X2

Invoice Number: 6120
Date: 2/28/20X2
Due Date: 3/30/20X2
Sales Order No: 2443

No. Ordered	Date Shipped	No. Shipped	No. left in order	Description	Price		Total
224	2/3/20X2	28	196	Carrot Cake	$2.40	μ	$67.20
426	2/3/20X2	53	373	Chocolate	$2.40		$127.20
134	2/3/20X2	17	117	Gluten-free Choc.	$2.40		$40.80
291	2/3/20X2	36	255	Lemon	$2.40		$86.40
157	2/3/20X2	20	137	Red Velvet	$2.40		$48.00
157	2/3/20X2	20	137	Spice	$2.40		$48.00
785	2/3/20X2	98	687	Vanilla	$2.40		$235.20
67	2/3/20X2	8	59	Almond Vegan	$2.40		$19.20
				Shipment Total			**$672.00**
224	2/6/20X2	28	168	Carrot Cake	$2.40		$67.20
426	2/6/20X2	53	320	Chocolate	$2.40		$127.20
134	2/6/20X2	17	100	Gluten-free Choc.	$2.40		$40.80
291	2/6/20X2	36	219	Lemon	$2.40		$86.40
157	2/6/20X2	20	117	Red Velvet	$2.40		$48.00
157	2/6/20X2	20	117	Spice	$2.40		$48.00
785	2/6/20X2	98	589	Vanilla	$2.40		$235.20
67	2/6/20X2	8	51	Almond Vegan	$2.40		$19.20
				Shipment Total			**$672.00**
224	2/10/20X2	28	140	Carrot Cake	$2.40		$67.20
426	2/10/20X2	53	267	Chocolate	$2.40		$127.20
134	2/10/20X2	17	83	Gluten-free Choc.	$2.40		$40.80
291	2/10/20X2	36	183	Lemon	$2.40		$86.40
157	2/10/20X2	20	97	Red Velvet	$2.40		$48.00
157	2/10/20X2	20	97	Spice	$2.40		$48.00
785	2/10/20X2	98	491	Vanilla	$2.40		$235.20
67	2/10/20X2	8	43	Almond Vegan	$2.40		$19.20
				Shipment Total			**$672.00**

Client Supporting Document

AR.2.4: pg. 3 of 11

PRODUCT INVOICE (continued)

Alpine Cupcakes, Inc.
1250 16th Street
Denver, Colorado 80202

Page 2/4

Shipped To:

High Country Coffee

3900 @ 32nd Street

Denver, CO 80212

Invoice Number: 6120

Date: 2/28/20X2

Ordered	Date Shipped	No. Shipped		No. left in order	Description	Price		Total
224	2/13/20X2	28	√	112	Carrot Cake	$2.40	μ	$67.20
426	2/13/20X2	53		214	Chocolate	$2.40		$127.20
134	2/13/20X2	17		66	Gluten-free Choc.	$2.40		$40.80
291	2/13/20X2	36		147	Lemon	$2.40		$86.40
157	2/13/20X2	20		77	Red Velvet	$2.40		$48.00
157	2/13/20X2	20		77	Spice	$2.40		$48.00
785	2/13/20X2	98		393	Vanilla	$2.40		$235.20
67	2/13/20X2	8		35	Almond Vegan	$2.40		$19.20
					Shipment Total			**$672.00**
224	2/17/20X2	28		84	Carrot Cake	$2.40		$67.20
426	2/17/20X2	53		161	Chocolate	$2.40		$127.20
134	2/17/20X2	17		49	Gluten-free Choc.	$2.40		$40.80
291	2/17/20X2	36		111	Lemon	$2.40		$86.40
157	2/17/20X2	20		57	Red Velvet	$2.40		$48.00
157	2/17/20X2	20		57	Spice	$2.40		$48.00
785	2/17/20X2	98		295	Vanilla	$2.40		$235.20
67	2/17/20X2	8		27	Almond Vegan	$2.40		$19.20
					Shipment Total			**$672.00**
224	2/20/20X2	28		56	Carrot Cake	$2.40		$67.20
426	2/20/20X2	53		108	Chocolate	$2.40		$127.20
134	2/20/20X2	17		32	Gluten-free Choc.	$2.40		$40.80
291	2/20/20X2	36		75	Lemon	$2.40		$86.40
157	2/20/20X2	20		37	Red Velvet	$2.40		$48.00
157	2/20/20X2	20		37	Spice	$2.40		$48.00
785	2/20/20X2	98		197	Vanilla	$2.40		$235.20
67	2/20/20X2	8		19	Almond Vegan	$2.40		$19.20
					Shipment Total			**$672.00**

Performed by:
TES 01/23/20X3
Reviewed by:
SDM 1/29/20x3

PRODUCT INVOICE (continued)

Alpine Cupcakes, Inc.
1250 16th Street
Denver, Colorado 80202

Page 3/4
Invoice Number: 6120
Date: 2/28/20X2

Shipped To:

High Country Coffee

3900 @ 32nd Street

Denver, CO 80212

Ordered	Date Shipped	No. Shipped	No. left in order	Description	Price	Total
224	2/24/20X2	28 √	28	Carrot Cake	$2.40 μ	$67.20
426	2/24/20X2	53	55	Chocolate	$2.40	$127.20
134	2/24/20X2	17	15	Gluten-free Choc.	$2.40	$40.80
291	2/24/20X2	36	39	Lemon	$2.40	$86.40
157	2/24/20X2	20	17	Red Velvet	$2.40	$48.00
157	2/24/20X2	20	17	Spice	$2.40	$48.00
785	2/24/20X2	98	99	Vanilla	$2.40	$235.20
67	2/24/20X2	8	11	Almond Vegan	$2.40	$19.20
				Shipment Total		$672.00
224	2/27/20X2	28	0	Carrot Cake	$2.40	$67.20
426	2/27/20X2	55	0	Chocolate	$2.40	$132.00
134	2/27/20X2	15	0	Gluten-free Choc.	$2.40	$36.00
291	2/27/20X2	39	0	Lemon	$2.40	$93.60
157	2/27/20X2	17	0	Red Velvet	$2.40	$40.80
157	2/27/20X2	17	0	Spice	$2.40	$40.80
67	2/27/20X2	11	0	Almond Vegan	$2.40	$26.40
				Shipment Total		**$674.40**

See Note A

Sales Tax	N/A
Freight	N/A
Invoice Total	$5,378.40

Tickmark Legend: √ - tied quantity between documents   μ - tied price between documents

Note A: For the last shipment of the month, the Vanilla cupcakes did not print on the invoice. The correct quantities were shipped to the customer and the customer was billed and paid the correct dollar amount. According to Miguel Lopez, they had a "snafu" in the invoicing software that caused it to omit printing the Vanilla cupcakes on the invoice. Miguel says the "snafu" has been fixed. Because the customer was shipped and billed correctly in total, this is not an exception. See Note 1 at AR 2.2.

Alpine Cupcakes, Inc.
High Country Coffee TOC Documents
Audit Year December 31, 20X2

Performed by:
TES 01/23/20X3
Reviewed by:
SDM 1/29/20x3

Please return this page with your payment

PRODUCT INVOICE

Remittance Advice

High Country Coffee
3900 @ 32nd Street
Denver, CO 80212

Page 4/4

Invoice Number:	6120
Sales Order No:	2443
Customer PO:	7915
Customer PO Date:	2/1/20X2
Amount Due:	$5,378.40
Date Due:	3/30/20X2

Date Paid _____
Amount Paid _____

Pmt Received 3/30/20X2

Lindsay McKenna
See returned remittance form

Performed by:
TES 01/23/20X3
Reviewed by:
SDM 1/29/20x3

ALPINE CUPCAKES, INC.
Shipping Report

Date: 2/3/20X2
Purchase Order #: 7915
Shipped To: High Country Coffee
Freight Carrier: Alpine Cupcake Carrier

Shipping Report # 24370

Quantity		Unit	Description
28	√	Cupcakes	Carrot Cake
53		Cupcakes	Chocolate
17		Cupcakes	Gluten-free Chocolate
36		Cupcakes	Lemon
20		Cupcakes	Red Velvet
20		Cupcakes	Spice
98		Cupcakes	Vanilla
8		Cupcakes	Almond Vegan

Remarks: _Items received in OK condition_____

Received By: __ Elaine' Mackay_____

Delivered To: __Receiving Dept._

ALPINE CUPCAKES, INC.
Shipping Report

Date: 2/6/20X2
Purchase Order #: 7915
Shipped To: High Country Coffee
Freight Carrier: Alpine Cupcake Carrier

Shipping Report # 24402

Quantity		Unit	Description
28	√	Cupcakes	Carrot Cake
53		Cupcakes	Chocolate
17		Cupcakes	Gluten-free Chocolate
36		Cupcakes	Lemon
20		Cupcakes	Red Velvet
20		Cupcakes	Spice
98		Cupcakes	Vanilla
8		Cupcakes	Almond Vegan

Remarks: _Items received in OK condition_____

Received By: __ Elaine' Mackay_____

Delivered To: __Receiving Dept._

Performed by:
TES 01/23/20X3
Reviewed by:
SDM 1/29/20x3

ALPINE CUPCAKES, INC.
Shipping Report

Date:	2/10/20X2		
Purchase Order #:	7915		**Shipping Report # 24456**
Shipped To:	High Country Coffee		
Freight Carrier:	Alpine Cupcake Carrier		

Quantity		Unit	Description
28	√	Cupcakes	Carrot Cake
53		Cupcakes	Chocolate
17		Cupcakes	Gluten-free Chocolate
36		Cupcakes	Lemon
20		Cupcakes	Red Velvet
20		Cupcakes	Spice
98		Cupcakes	Vanilla
8		Cupcakes	Almond Vegan

Remarks: _Items received in OK condition_

Received By: _Elaine' Mackay_

Delivered To: _Receiving Dept._

ALPINE CUPCAKES, INC.
Shipping Report

Date:	2/13/20X2		
Purchase Order #:	7915		**Shipping Report # 24523**
Shipped To:	High Country Coffee		
Freight Carrier:	Alpine Cupcake Carrier		

Quantity		Unit	Description
28	√	Cupcakes	Carrot Cake
53		Cupcakes	Chocolate
17		Cupcakes	Gluten-free Chocolate
36		Cupcakes	Lemon
20		Cupcakes	Red Velvet
20		Cupcakes	Spice
98		Cupcakes	Vanilla
8		Cupcakes	Almond Vegan

Remarks: _Items received in OK condition_

Received By: _Elaine' Mackay_

Delivered To: _Receiving Dept._

Performed by:
TES 01/23/20X3
Reviewed by:
SDM 1/29/20x3

ALPINE CUPCAKES, INC.
Shipping Report

Date: 2/17/20X2

Purchase Order #: 7915

Shipped To: High Country Coffee

Freight Carrier: Alpine Cupcake Carrier

Shipping Report # 24578

Quantity		Unit	Description
28	√	Cupcakes	Carrot Cake
53		Cupcakes	Chocolate
17		Cupcakes	Gluten-free Chocolate
36		Cupcakes	Lemon
20		cupcakes	Red Velvet
20		cupcakes	Spice
98		cupcakes	Vanilla
8		cupcakes	Almond Vegan

Remarks: *Items received in OK condition*

Received By: *Elaine' Mackay*

Delivered To: *Receiving Dept.*

ALPINE CUPCAKES, INC.
Shipping Report

Date: 2/20/20X2

Purchase Order #: 7915

Shipped To: High Country Coffee

Freight Carrier: Alpine Cupcake Carrier

Shipping Report # 24598

Quantity		Unit	Description
28	√	Cupcakes	Carrot Cake
53		Cupcakes	Chocolate
17		Cupcakes	Gluten-free Chocolate
36		Cupcakes	Lemon
20		Cupcakes	Red Velvet
20		Cupcakes	Spice
98		Cupcakes	Vanilla
8		Cupcakes	Almond Vegan

Remarks: *Items received in OK condition*

Received By: *Elaine' Mackay*

Delivered To: *Receiving Dept.*

Performed by:
TES 01/23/20X3
Reviewed by:
SDM 1/29/20X3

ALPINE CUPCAKES, INC.

Shipping Report

Date: 3/1/20X2

Purchase Order #: 7915

Shipped To: High Country Coffee

Freight Carrier: Alpine Cupcake Carrier

Shipping Report # 24624

Quantity		Unit	Description
28	√	Cupcakes	Carrot Cake
53		Cupcakes	Chocolate
17		Cupcakes	Gluten-free Chocolate
36		Cupcakes	Lemon
20		Cupcakes	Red Velvet
20		Cupcakes	Spice
98		Cupcakes	Vanilla
8		Cupcakes	Almond Vegan

Remarks: *Items received in OK condition*

Received By: *Elaine' Mackay*

Delivered To: *Receiving Dept.*

ALPINE CUPCAKES, INC.

Shipping Report

Date: 3/4/20X2

Purchase Order #: 7915

Shipped To: High Country Coffee

Freight Carrier: Alpine Cupcake Carrier

Shipping Report # 24681

Quantity		Unit	Description
28	√	Cupcakes	Carrot Cake
55		Cupcakes	Chocolate
15		Cupcakes	Gluten-free Chocolate
39		Cupcakes	Lemon
17		Cupcakes	Red Velvet
17		Cupcakes	Spice
99		Cupcakes	Vanilla
11		Cupcakes	Almond Vegan

Remarks: *Items received in OK condition*

Received By: *Elaine' Mackay*

Delivered To: *Receiving Dept.*

Tickmark Legend: √ - *tied quantity between documents* μ - *tied price between documents*

Performed by:
TES 01/23/20X3
Reviewed by:
SDM 1/29/20x3

Please return this page with your payment

PRODUCT INVOICE

Remittance Advice

High Country Coffee

3900 @ 32nd Street

Denver, CO 80212

Page 4/4

Invoice Number:	6120
Sales Order No:	2443
Customer PO:	7915
Customer PO Date:	2/1/20X2
Amount Due:	$5,378.40
Date Due:	3/30/20X2

Date Paid   3/30/20X2

Amount Paid $5,378.40   μ

Tickmark Legend:

√ – *tied quantity between documents*

μ – *tied price between documents*

PMT RECEIVED
3/30/20X2

Lindsay McKenna

Garcia and Foster, CPAs

Performed By: *TES*   **Reviewed By:** SDM
Date: *02/10/20X3*   **Date:** 2/12/20x3

Client: Alpine Cupcakes, Inc.
Year End: 12/31/20X2

We analyzed the AR and sales account balances and performed ratio analysis of the 12/31/20X2 balances and activity. See AR.3.2 –AR.3.4 for analysis. Per our firm methodology, we identified any significant fluctuation in account balances from the prior year as a change of over 25% of TM ($3,700 \times 25\% = \$925$) and over a 4% change. For the ratio analysis, our firm methodology is to investigate ratio changes from the prior year that are over a 4% change.

For substantiating the fluctuations in sales revenue, our firm methodology is to look at specific customer accounts that had a change greater than $6,000. In order to substantiate sales to these customers, we reviewed supporting documentation to validate the sales transactions to these customers. See AR.3.4 for more details.

Performed by:
TES 02/10/20X3
Reviewed by:
SDM 2/12/20x3

AR and Sales Related Account Analysis:

Account	Total Balance 12/31/X1	Total Balance 12/31/X2	$ Change	% Change
Sales Revenue: Corporate Accounts *PY*	$1,400,349.58	$1,465,488.42 *TB*	$65,138.84	4.65% ✓
Sales Revenue: Storefront	345,317.00	348,820.50	3,503.50	1.01% ✓
Total Sales Revenue	**$1,745,666.58**	**$1,815,308.93**		
	7	7		
COGS: Ingredients	264,716.87	275,649.21 *TB*	10,932.34	4.13%
COGS: Boxes and Cupcake Cups	15,389.90	16,093.95	704.05	4.57%
COGS: Beverages	23,081.20	23,390.80	309.60	1.34%
Total COGS	**$303,187.97**	**$315,133.96**		
	7	7		
Accounts Receivable	**$191,451.64**	**$195,120.87** *TB*	**$3,669.23**	1.92%
Allowance for Uncollectible Accounts	$0.00	$0.00	$0.00	0.00%

Ratio Analysis:

	12/31/20X1 Ratio	12/31/20X2 Ratio	% Change
AR Turnover = Net Credit Sales / Avg. AR	10.13	7.58	-27%
Days Sales Outstanding = 365/AR Turnover	35.39	48.14	36%
Gross Margin % = (Sales – COGS)/Sales	0.83	0.83	0%

Product Analysis (Number Sold):

	20X1	20X2	% Change
Total Cupcakes	653,347	682,514	4.46%
Coffee	33,063	32,775	-0.87%
Sodas	31,240	30,418	-2.63%
Hot Chocolate	11,466	11,573	0.93%
Milk	16,484	17,013	3.21%

Garcia and Foster Audit Workpaper

AR.3.2: pg. 1 of 2

Performed by:
TES 02/10/20X3
Reviewed by:
SDM 2/12/20x3

Auditor Notes

TB - Agreed to December Trial Balance.

PY- Agreed to PY workpapers.

√ - The fluctuation is less than 25% of TM ($925) and less than a 4% change.

μ - The ratio fluctuation is less than a 4% change.

F – Footed

1 – Per discussion with Lisa Mercer, the company has seen a significant increase in several customers' sales during 20X2. The following customers all had an increase in sales revenue from 20X1 of over $6,000: Bon Appetito Restaurants, Elkhorn Coffee Shops, High Country Coffee, Julie's Wraps. Increase in sales leads to the increased shipping revenue as the revenue is charged on a per cupcake basis. See AR.3.3

2 - Per discussion with Lisa Mercer, Alpine Cupcakes does a careful credit check of customers prior to issuing credit, and they have not had a problem collecting in the past. Were they to have a customer who did not pay, they would use the direct write-off method to eliminate the receivable. ← √

3 - Per discussion with Lisa Mercer, the collection of AR balances is within industry standards.

4 - Per discussion with Lisa Mercer, Alpine Cupcakes experienced increased customers' sales in 20X2. These changes also led to increases in the number of cupcakes being sold. See AR.3.3 and AR.3.4. √

Alpine Cupcakes, Inc.
20X2 Cupcake Corporate Sales Analysis
Audit Year December 31, 20X2

	Performed by:
	TES 02/10/20X3
	Reviewed by:
	SDM 2/12/20x3

Customer Name	20X1 Cupcakes Ordered	20X1 Invoice Total	20X2 Cupcakes Ordered	20X2 Invoice Total	Change Cupcakes Ordered	$ Change Invoice Total	
Bon Appetito Restaurants	**59,493**	**142,783.20**	**62,088**	**149,011.20**	**2,595**	**6,228.00**	1
Boulder Tea House	5,095	12,228.00	4,464	10,713.60	(631)	(1,514.40)	✓
Broken Eggs Restaurant	7,052	16,924.80	7,150	17,160.00	98	235.20	
Brown's Tavern	5,694	13,665.60	4,225	10,140.00	(1,469)	(3,525.60)	
Bubba's Fish House	9,622	23,092.80	10,485	25,164.00	863	2,071.20	
Buckhead Restaurants	13,057	31,336.80	14,913	35,791.20	1,856	4,454.40	
Chavez Cantina	14,016	33,638.40	15,842	38,020.80	1,826	4,382.40	
Country Barrel Restaurants	35,419	85,005.60	35,044	84,105.60	(375)	(900.00)	
Denver Bakery Café	22,809	54,741.60	24,259	58,221.60	1,450	3,480.00	
Denver Sirloin Restaurants	19,529	46,869.60	18,578	44,587.20	(951)	(2,282.40)	
Elkhorn Coffee Shops	**31,674**	**76,017.60**	**34,449**	**82,677.60**	**2,775**	**6,660.00**	1
Fontana Catering & Café	15,210	36,504.00	16,067	38,560.80	857	2,056.80	✓
Granny's Café	13,766	33,038.40	13,994	33,585.60	228	547.20	
High Country Coffee	**23,784**	**57,081.60**	**27,365**	**65,676.00**	**3,581**	**8,594.40**	1
Julie's Wraps	**7,602**	**18,244.80**	**10,613**	**25,471.20**	**3,011**	**7,226.40**	
Little's Grill	5,608	13,459.20	6,218	14,923.20	610	1,464.00	✓
Luigi's Bistro	8,396	20,150.40	6,683	16,039.20	(1,713)	(4,111.20)	
Mile High Steakhouses	44,794	107,505.60	45,569	109,365.60	775	1,860.00	
Mountain Lion Restaurant	10,235	24,564.00	10,429	25,029.60	194	465.60	
Mountain Trout Fish House	11,391	27,338.40	12,269	29,445.60	878	2,107.20	
Nora's Café	17,922	43,012.80	20,005	48,012.00	2,083	4,999.20	
Papa's Restaurant	12,677	30,424.80	13,496	32,390.40	819	1,965.60	
Pebbles Inn	4,310	10,344.00	3,520	8,448.00	(790)	(1,896.00)	
Scotty's Taverns	6,079	14,589.60	6,288	15,091.20	209	501.60	
Smokey's Barbeque Pit	**14,005**	**33,612.00**	**17,530**	**42,072.00**	**3,525**	**8,460.00**	1
Southside Café	9,304	22,329.60	9,364	22,473.60	60	144.00	✓
St. Francis Hotel and Spa	13,449	32,277.60	15,655	37,572.00	2,206	5,294.40	
Steinberg Delis	10,752	25,804.80	9,265	22,236.00	(1,487)	(3,568.80)	
The Breakfast Place	18,984	45,561.60	20,544	49,305.60	1,560	3,744.00	
The Sandwich Place	4,474	10,737.60	5,287	12,688.80	813	1,951.20	
UC Boulder Food Service	58,948	141,475.20	58,118	139,483.20	(830)	(1,992.00)	
UC Denver Food Service	44,305	106,332.00	46,633	111,919.20	2,328	5,587.20	
Cupcake Sales Revenue	579,455	1,390,692.00	606,409	1,455,381.60			
Shipping Revenue		9,657.52		10,106.82			
Corporate Sales Revenue	*AR.3.2*	1,400,349.52	*AR.3.2*	1,465,488.42			
		F		*F*			

Garcia and Foster Audit Workpaper

AR.3.3: pg. 1 of 2

134

Performed by:
TES 02/10/20X3
Reviewed by:
SDM 2/12/20x3

Auditor Notes

TB - Agreed to December Trial Balance.

PY - Agreed to PY workpapers.

i - immaterial

✓ - The fluctuation is less than $6,000

F — Footed

1 —Any fluctuations of the customer's dollar value of cupcakes sold that were greater than $6,000 were substantiated by obtaining and reviewing all sales invoices, shipping documents, and customer purchase orders for 20X2. We calculated the total sales and total number of cupcakes sold from supporting documents. See AR.3.4

Alpine Cupcakes, Inc.
20X2 Monthly Sales Analysis
Audit Year December 31, 20X2

Performed by:
TES 02/10/20X3
Reviewed by:
SDM 2/12/20x3

Customer Name	Monthly Sales	20X2 Total Cupcakes Ordered	20X2 Invoice Total	
Bon Appetito Restaurants	January	4,049	9,717.60	✓
Bon Appetito Restaurants	February	5,508	13,219.20	
Bon Appetito Restaurants	March	4,572	10,972.80	
Bon Appetito Restaurants	April	4,390	10,536.00	
Bon Appetito Restaurants	May	3,519	8,445.60	
Bon Appetito Restaurants	June	6,300	15,120.00	
Bon Appetito Restaurants	July	5,484	13,161.60	
Bon Appetito Restaurants	August	6,267	15,040.80	
Bon Appetito Restaurants	September	4,692	11,260.80	
Bon Appetito Restaurants	October	4,570	10,968.00	
Bon Appetito Restaurants	November	5,667	13,600.80	
Bon Appetito Restaurants	**TOTAL**	**62,088**	**149,011.20**	*AR.3.3*
Elkhorn Coffee Shops	January	2,892	6,940.80	
Elkhorn Coffee Shops	February	2,873	6,895.20	
Elkhorn Coffee Shops	March	1,977	4,744.80	
Elkhorn Coffee Shops	April	2,678	6,427.20	
Elkhorn Coffee Shops	May	2,052	4,924.80	
Elkhorn Coffee Shops	June	3,038	7,291.20	
Elkhorn Coffee Shops	July	3,487	8,368.80	
Elkhorn Coffee Shops	August	3,153	7,567.20	
Elkhorn Coffee Shops	September	2,131	5,114.40	
Elkhorn Coffee Shops	October	3,322	7,972.80	
Elkhorn Coffee Shops	November	2,486	5,966.40	
Elkhorn Coffee Shops	December	4,360	10,464.00	
Elkhorn Coffee Shops	**TOTAL**	**34,449**	**82,677.60**	*AR.3.3*
High Country Coffee	January	2,292	5,500.80	
High Country Coffee	February	2,241	5,378.40	
High Country Coffee	March	2,172	5,212.80	
High Country Coffee	April	1,502	3,604.80	
High Country Coffee	May	1,468	3,523.20	
High Country Coffee	June	2,904	6,969.60	
High Country Coffee	July	2,388	5,731.20	
High Country Coffee	August	3,464	8,313.60	
High Country Coffee	September	1,757	4,216.80	
High Country Coffee	October	2,022	4,852.80	
High Country Coffee	November	2,736	6,566.40	
High Country Coffee	December	2,419	5,805.60	
High Country Coffee	**TOTAL**	**27,365**	**65,676.00**	*AR.3.3*

Garcia and Foster Audit Workpaper

AR.3.4: pg. 1 of 2

Alpine Cupcakes, Inc.
20X2 Monthly Sales Analysis
Audit Year December 31, 20X2

Performed by:
TES 02/10/20X3
Reviewed by:
SDM 2/12/20x3

Customer Name	Monthly Sales	20X2 Total Cupcakes Ordered	20X2 Invoice Total	
Julie's Wraps	January	925	2,220.00	✓
Julie's Wraps	February	1,251	3,002.40	
Julie's Wraps	March	872	2,092.80	
Julie's Wraps	April	936	2,246.40	
Julie's Wraps	May	463	1,111.20	
Julie's Wraps	June	1,367	3,280.80	
Julie's Wraps	July	1,143	2,743.20	
Julie's Wraps	August	609	1,461.60	
Julie's Wraps	September	678	1,627.20	
Julie's Wraps	October	692	1,660.80	
Julie's Wraps	November	1,006	2,414.40	
Julie's Wraps	December	671	1,610.40	
Julie's Wraps	**TOTAL**	**10,613**	**25,471.20**	AR.3.3
Smokey's Barbeque Pit	January	1,050	2,520.00	
Smokey's Barbeque Pit	February	1,935	4,644.00	
Smokey's Barbeque Pit	March	1,109	2,661.60	
Smokey's Barbeque Pit	April	758	1,819.20	
Smokey's Barbeque Pit	May	1,263	3,031.20	
Smokey's Barbeque Pit	June	1,788	4,291.20	
Smokey's Barbeque Pit	July	1,032	2,476.80	
Smokey's Barbeque Pit	August	2,177	5,224.80	
Smokey's Barbeque Pit	September	841	2,018.40	
Smokey's Barbeque Pit	October	1,850	4,440.00	
Smokey's Barbeque Pit	November	1,743	4,183.20	
Smokey's Barbeque Pit	December	1,984	4,761.60	
Smokey's Barbeque Pit	**TOTAL**	**17,530**	**42,072.00**	AR.3.3
		F	F	

Auditor Notes

F – Footed

✓ –We obtained all monthly supporting documents for customers that had a change in sales from 20X2 that were greater than $6,000. To validate the sales for 20X2, we reviewed all sales invoices, shipping documents, and customer purchase orders for these customers. We calculated the total sales and total number of cupcakes sold from supporting documents. The total number of cupcakes sold and total dollar value of sales ties to AR.3.3 for each customer. No exceptions noted.

Garcia and Foster Audit Workpaper

AR.3.4: pg. 2 of 2

Alpine Cupcakes, Inc.
20X2 AR Aging Auditor Memo
Audit Year December 31, 20X2

Garcia and Foster, CPAs

Performed By: *TES*   **Reviewed By:** SDM
Date: *02/12/20X3*   **Date:** 2/14/20X3

Client: Alpine Cupcakes, Inc.
Year End: 12/31/20X2

We tested the aging of the Accounts Receivable balances to validate the accuracy of the company's AR aging report. By testing the aging categories, we can then determine the reasonableness of the net realizable value of the AR balance (accounts receivable less the allowance for uncollectible accounts). If the company has misclassified the age of AR balances, this can affect our estimate of the allowance for uncollectible accounts.

Audit Procedures Performed:
1. Traced the totals of the AR 20X2 and AR 20X1 total balance to the AR Lead Sheet balances.
2. Compared the 20X2 AR aging categories to the 20X1 AR aging categories to determine any significant fluctuations.
3. Randomly selected 3 account balances from each aging category to substantively test the placement of accounts into the proper aging categories. Compared the dates on the product invoice, shipping invoice, and shipping report to validate the accuracy of the aging category.

Customer Name	Aging Category	Date of Product Invoice	Dates in Shipping Invoice	Dates in Shipping Reports	Proper Aging Group (Y/N)	
Denver Bakery Café	Past Due 31–60 days	11/30/20X2	11/1/20X2 to 11/25/20X2	11/1/20X2 to 11/25/20X2	Yes	*AR.4.3*
Luigi's Bistro	Past Due 61–90 days	10/31/20X2	10/5/20X2 to 10/29/20X2	10/5/20X2 to 10/29/20X2	Yes	*AR.4.4*
Buckhead Restaurants	Past Due 91–120 days	9/30/20X2	9/3/20X2 to 9/30/20X2	9/3/20X2 to 9/30/20X2	Yes	*AR.4.5*

The company makes multiple shipments to customers throughout the month and then bills each customer at the end of the month. Sales are not recorded on the date that the goods are shipped; however, the aging categories are accurate based on all shipments being made within the aging category. In our audit procedures, we did not find any material misstatements and the AR Aging Report categories appear to be appropriately classified.

Alpine Cupcakes, Inc.
20X2 AR Aging Schedule
Audit Year December 31, 20X2

Performed by:
TES 02/12/20X3
Reviewed by:
SDM 2/14/20X3

Customer Name	Total Balance	Current 0–30	Past Due 31–60	Past Due 61–90	Past Due 91–120	120 days past due
Bon Appetito Restaurants AR.5.3	$17,085.83	$17,085.83	$0.00	$0.00	$0.00	$0.00
Boulder Tea House	582.42	582.42	0.00	0.00	0.00	0.00
Broken Eggs Restaurant	2,177.42	2,177.42	0.00	0.00	0.00	0.00
Brown's Tavern	691.92	451.92	240.00	0.00	0.00	0.00
Bubba's Fish House	1,227.67	1,227.67	0.00	0.00	0.00	0.00
Buckhead Restaurants AR.5.5	12,147.95	2,660.75	3,964.80	3,669.60	1,852.80 *x*	0.00
Chavez Cantina	4,753.58	4,753.58	0.00	0.00	0.00	0.00
Country Barrel Restaurants	8,511.50	8,511.50	0.00	0.00	0.00	0.00
Denver Bakery Café	10,785.59	5,831.42	4,954.17 *x*	0.00	0.00	0.00
Denver Sirloin Restaurants	8,233.20	4,698.00	3,535.20	0.00	0.00	0.00
Elkhorn Coffee Shops	10,536.67	10,536.67	0.00	0.00	0.00	0.00
Fontana Catering & Café	3,458.25	3,458.25	0.00	0.00	0.00	0.00
Granny's Café	3,770.00	3,770.00	0.00	0.00	0.00	0.00
High Country Coffee	5,891.52	5,845.92	45.60	0.00	0.00	0.00
Julie's Wraps	1,621.58	1,621.58	0.00	0.00	0.00	0.00
Little's Grill	2,081.47	1,140.67	940.80	0.00	0.00	0.00
Luigi's Bistro	5,083.97	1,503.17	2,380.80	1,200.00 *x*	0.00	0.00
Mile High Steakhouses AR.5.2	20,550.57	11,392.17	9,158.40	0.00	0.00	0.00
Mountain Lion Restaurant	3,400.25	3,400.25	0.00	0.00	0.00	0.00
Mountain Trout Fish House	3,458.25	3,458.25	0.00	0.00	0.00	0.00
Nora's Café	9,364.45	4,473.25	4,891.20	0.00	0.00	0.00
Papa's Restaurant	3,216.58	3,216.58	0.00	0.00	0.00	0.00
Pebbles Inn	2,029.32	1,582.92	446.40	0.00	0.00	0.00
Scotty's Taverns	2,658.18	2,288.58	369.60	0.00	0.00	0.00
Smokey's Barbeque Pit	8,977.87	4,794.67	4,183.20	0.00	0.00	0.00
Southside Café	1,307.42	1,307.42	0.00	0.00	0.00	0.00
St. Francis Hotel and Spa	5,642.92	5,642.92	0.00	0.00	0.00	0.00
Steinberg Delis	3,859.32	2,104.92	1,754.40	0.00	0.00	0.00
The Breakfast Place	4,144.58	4,144.58	0.00	0.00	0.00	0.00
The Sandwich Place AR.5.6	2,432.20	841.00	1,591.20	0.00	0.00	0.00
UC Boulder Food Service AR.5.4	14,761.00	14,761.00	0.00	0.00	0.00	0.00
UC Denver Food Service	11,447.75	11,447.75	0.00	0.00	0.00	0.00
20X2 Total Balance	$195,891.20	$150,713.03	$38,455.77	$4,869.60	$1,852.80	$0.00
20X1 Total Balance	$192,221.91	$155,223.15	$35,153.16	$1,845.60	$0.00	$0.00
$ Difference from 20X1	$3,669.29	-$4,510.12	$3,302.61	$3,024.00	$1,852.80	
% Change from 20X1	1.91%	-2.91%	9.39%	163.85%	100.00%	

Performed by:
TES 02/12/20X3
Reviewed by:
SDM 2/14/20X3

Auditor Notes

✓ – *The fluctuation is less than TM ($3,000) and less than a 10% change.*

F – *Footed*

1 – *In tying out the current year and prior year AR balances to the lead sheet (AR.3.2), we found a difference between current year and prior year numbers. Each year has a difference of $770.27. Per discussion with Lisa Mercer, this is due to the company not properly recording AR entries in 20X0. The company plans to clean this up in 20X3 to make the proper adjusting entries. This amount needs to be written off as these are old balances that were never invoiced to the customers. This amount is immaterial.*

X – *We randomly selected 3 account balances to test the classification of the transactions into the proper aging category. In each transaction, we compared the dates in the aging to the dates in the product invoice, shipping invoice, and shipping reports. All transactions appear to be properly classified.*

Performed by:
TES 02/12/20X3
Reviewed by:
SDM 2/14/20x3

PRODUCT INVOICE

Alpine Cupcakes, Inc.
1250 16th Street
Denver, Colorado 80202

Page 1/4

Shipped To:

Denver Bakery Café
321 17th Street
Denver, CO 80202

Customer PO: 1117
Customer PO Date: 11/1/20X2

AR.4.1 Date: 11/30/20X2
Invoice Number: 6412
Due Date: 12/30/20X2
Sales Order No: 2735

No. Ordered	Date Shipped	No. Shipped	No. Left in Order	Description	Price	Total
267	11/1/20X2	33	234	Carrot Cake	$2.40	$79.20
451	11/1/20X2	56	395	Chocolate	$2.40	$134.40
184	11/1/20X2	23	161	Gluten-free Choc.	$2.40	$55.20
328	11/1/20X2	41	287	Lemon	$2.40	$98.40
123	11/1/20X2	15	108	Red Velvet	$2.40	$36.00
164	11/1/20X2	21	143	Spice	$2.40	$50.40
451	11/1/20X2	56	395	Vanilla	$2.40	$134.40
82	11/1/20X2	10	72	Almond Vegan	$2.40	$24.00
				Total Shipment		**$612.00**
267	11/4/20X2	33	201	Carrot Cake	$2.40	$79.20
451	11/4/20X2	56	339	Chocolate	$2.40	$134.40
184	11/4/20X2	23	138	Gluten-free Choc.	$2.40	$55.20
328	11/4/20X2	41	246	Lemon	$2.40	$98.40
123	11/4/20X2	15	93	Red Velvet	$2.40	$36.00
164	11/4/20X2	21	122	Spice	$2.40	$50.40
451	11/4/20X2	56	339	Vanilla	$2.40	$134.40
82	11/4/20X2	10	62	Almond Vegan	$2.40	$24.00
				Total Shipment		**$612.00**
267	11/7/20X2	33	168	Carrot Cake	$2.40	$79.20
451	11/7/20X2	56	283	Chocolate	$2.40	$134.40
184	11/7/20X2	23	115	Gluten-free Choc.	$2.40	$55.20
328	11/7/20X2	41	205	Lemon	$2.40	$98.40
123	11/7/20X2	15	78	Red Velvet	$2.40	$36.00
164	11/7/20X2	21	101	Spice	$2.40	$50.40
451	11/7/20X2	56	283	Vanilla	$2.40	$134.40
82	11/7/20X2	10	52	Almond Vegan	$2.40	$24.00
				Total Shipment		**$612.00**

Client Supporting Document

AR.4.3: pg. 1 of 12

Performed by:
TES 02/12/20X3
Reviewed by:
SDM 2/14/20x3

PRODUCT INVOICE (continued)

Alpine Cupcakes, Inc.
1250 16th Street
Denver, Colorado 80202

Page 2/4
Invoice Number: 6412
Date: 11/30/20X2

Shipped To:

Denver Bakery Café
321 17th Street
Denver, CO 80202

Ordered	Date Shipped	No. Shipped	No. Left in Order	Description	Price	Total
267	11/10/20X2	33	135	Carrot Cake	$2.40	$79.20
451	11/10/20X2	56	227	Chocolate	$2.40	$134.40
184	11/10/20X2	23	92	Gluten-free Choc.	$2.40	$55.20
328	11/10/20X2	41	164	Lemon	$2.40	$98.40
123	11/10/20X2	15	63	Red Velvet	$2.40	$36.00
164	11/10/20X2	21	80	Spice	$2.40	$50.40
451	11/10/20X2	56	227	Vanilla	$2.40	$134.40
82	11/10/20X2	10	42	Almond Vegan	$2.40	$24.00
				Total Shipment		**$612.00**
267	11/14/20X2	33	102	Carrot Cake	$2.40	$79.20
451	11/14/20X2	56	171	Chocolate	$2.40	$134.40
184	11/14/20X2	23	69	Gluten-free Choc.	$2.40	$55.20
328	11/14/20X2	41	123	Lemon	$2.40	$98.40
123	11/14/20X2	15	48	Red Velvet	$2.40	$36.00
164	11/14/20X2	21	59	Spice	$2.40	$50.40
451	11/14/20X2	56	171	Vanilla	$2.40	$134.40
82	11/14/20X2	10	32	Almond Vegan	$2.40	$24.00
				Total Shipment		**$612.00**
267	11/17/20X2	33	69	Carrot Cake	$2.40	$79.20
451	11/17/20X2	56	115	Chocolate	$2.40	$134.40
184	11/17/20X2	23	46	Gluten-free Choc.	$2.40	$55.20
328	11/17/20X2	41	82	Lemon	$2.40	$98.40
123	11/17/20X2	15	33	Red Velvet	$2.40	$36.00
164	11/17/20X2	21	38	Spice	$2.40	$50.40
451	11/17/20X2	56	115	Vanilla	$2.40	$134.40
82	11/17/20X2	10	22	Almond Vegan	$2.40	$24.00
				Total Shipment		**$612.00**

Performed by:
TES 02/12/20X3
Reviewed by:
SDM 2/14/20x3

PRODUCT INVOICE (continued)

Alpine Cupcakes, Inc.
1250 16th Street
Denver, Colorado 80202

Page 3/4

Shipped To:

Denver Bakery Café

321 17th Street

Denver, CO 80202

Invoice Number: 6412

Date: 11/30/20X2

Ordered	Date Shipped	No. Shipped	No. Left in Order	Description	Price	Total
267	11/21/20X2	33	36	Carrot Cake	$2.40	$79.20
451	11/21/20X2	56	59	Chocolate	$2.40	$134.40
184	11/21/20X2	23	23	Gluten-free Choc.	$2.40	$55.20
328	11/21/20X2	41	41	Lemon	$2.40	$98.40
123	11/21/20X2	15	18	Red Velvet	$2.40	$36.00
164	11/21/20X2	21	17	Spice	$2.40	$50.40
451	11/21/20X2	56	59	Vanilla	$2.40	$134.40
82	11/21/20X2	10	12	Almond Vegan	$2.40	$24.00
				Total Shipment		**$612.00**
267	11/25/20X2	36	0	Carrot Cake	$2.40	$86.40
451	11/25/20X2	59	0	Chocolate	$2.40	$141.60
184	11/25/20X2	23	0	Gluten-free Choc.	$2.40	$55.20
328	11/25/20X2	41	0	Lemon	$2.40	$98.40
123	11/25/20X2	18	0	Red Velvet	$2.40	$43.20
164	11/25/20X2	17	0	Spice	$2.40	$40.80
451	11/25/20X2	59	0	Vanilla	$2.40	$141.60
82	11/25/20X2	12	0	Almond Vegan	$2.40	$28.80
				Total Shipment		**$636.00**

Sales Tax	N/A
Freight	N/A
Invoice Total	$4,920.00

Performed by:
TES 02/12/20X3
Reviewed by:
SDM 2/14/20X3

Please return this page with your payment

PRODUCT INVOICE

Remittance Advice

Denver Bakery Café
321 17th Street
Denver, CO 80202

Page 4/4

Invoice Number:	6412
Sales Order No:	2735
Customer PO:	1117
Customer PO Date:	11/1/20X2
Total amount Owed:	$4,920.00
Date Due:	12/30/20X2

Date Paid _____
Amount Paid _____

**Pmt Received
1/2/20X3**

Lindsay McKenna

See returned remittance form

Performed by:
TES 02/12/20X3
Reviewed by:
SDM 2/14/20x3

SHIPPING INVOICE

Alpine Cupcakes, Inc.
1250 16th Street
Denver, Colorado 80202

Page 1/4

Shipped To:

Denver Bakery Café

321 17th Street, Denver, CO 80202

Customer PO: 1117   Customer PO Date: 11/1/20X2

Ship Invoice Number: S6412

Date: 11/30/20X2

Due Date: 12/30/20X2

Sales Order No: 2735

Shipping Report # 27398

No. Ordered	Date Shipped	Dozen Shipped	Description	Price per Dozen	Total
267	*AR.4.1* 11/1/20X2	2.75	Carrot Cake	$0.20	$0.55
451	11/1/20X2	4.67	Chocolate	$0.20	$0.93
184	11/1/20X2	1.92	Gluten-free Choc.	$0.20	$0.38
328	11/1/20X2	3.42	Lemon	$0.20	$0.68
123	11/1/20X2	1.25	Red Velvet	$0.20	$0.25
164	11/1/20X2	1.75	Spice	$0.20	$0.35
451	11/1/20X2	4.67	Vanilla	$0.20	$0.93
82	11/1/20X2	0.83	Almond Vegan	$0.20	$0.17
	Total Shipped	**21.26**	**Price per Dozen**	**$0.20**	**$4.25**

Shipping Report # 27482

No. Ordered	Date Shipped	Dozen Shipped	Description	Price per Dozen	Total
267	11/4/20X2	2.75	Carrot Cake	$0.20	$0.55
451	11/4/20X2	4.67	Chocolate	$0.20	$0.93
184	11/4/20X2	1.92	Gluten-free Choc.	$0.20	$0.38
328	11/4/20X2	3.42	Lemon	$0.20	$0.68
123	11/4/20X2	1.25	Red Velvet	$0.20	$0.25
164	11/4/20X2	1.75	Spice	$0.20	$0.35
451	11/4/20X2	4.67	Vanilla	$0.20	$0.93
82	11/4/20X2	0.83	Almond Vegan	$0.20	$0.17
	Total Shipped	**21.26**	**Price per Dozen**	**$0.20**	**$4.25**

Shipping Report # 27501

No. Ordered	Date Shipped	Dozen Shipped	Description	Price per Dozen	Total
267	11/7/20X2	2.75	Carrot Cake	$0.20	$0.55
451	11/7/20X2	4.67	Chocolate	$0.20	$0.93
184	11/7/20X2	1.92	Gluten-free Choc.	$0.20	$0.38
328	11/7/20X2	3.42	Lemon	$0.20	$0.68
123	11/7/20X2	1.25	Red Velvet	$0.20	$0.25
164	11/7/20X2	1.75	Spice	$0.20	$0.35
451	11/7/20X2	4.67	Vanilla	$0.20	$0.93
82	11/7/20X2	0.83	Almond Vegan	$0.20	$0.17
	Total Shipped	**21.26**	**Price per Dozen**	**$0.20**	**$4.25**

Client Supporting Document   AR.4.3: pg. 5 of 12

Performed by:
TES 02/12/20X3
Reviewed by:
SDM 2/14/20x3

SHIPPING INVOICE (continued)

Alpine Cupcakes, Inc.
1250 16th Street
Denver, Colorado 80202

Page 2/4
Ship Invoice Number:
S6412

Date: 11/30/20X2

Shipped To:

Denver Bakery Café

321 17th Street

Denver, CO 80202

Shipping Report # 27578

Ordered		Date Shipped	Dozen Shipped	Description	Price per Dozen	Total
267	*AR.4.1*	11/10/20X2	2.75	Carrot Cake	$0.20	$0.55
451		11/10/20X2	4.67	Chocolate	$0.20	$0.93
184		11/10/20X2	1.92	Gluten-free Choc.	$0.20	$0.38
328		11/10/20X2	3.42	Lemon	$0.20	$0.68
123		11/10/20X2	1.25	Red Velvet	$0.20	$0.25
164		11/10/20X2	1.75	Spice	$0.20	$0.35
451		11/10/20X2	4.67	Vanilla	$0.20	$0.93
82		11/10/20X2	0.83	Almond Vegan	$0.20	$0.17
		Total Shipped	**21.26**	**Price per Dozen**	**$0.20**	**$4.25**

Shipping Report # 27614

Ordered	Date Shipped	Dozen Shipped	Description	Price per Dozen	Total
267	11/14/20X2	2.75	Carrot Cake	$0.20	$0.55
451	11/14/20X2	4.67	Chocolate	$0.20	$0.93
184	11/14/20X2	1.92	Gluten-free Choc.	$0.20	$0.38
328	11/14/20X2	3.42	Lemon	$0.20	$0.68
123	11/14/20X2	1.25	Red Velvet	$0.20	$0.25
164	11/14/20X2	1.75	Spice	$0.20	$0.35
451	11/14/20X2	4.67	Vanilla	$0.20	$0.93
82	11/14/20X2	0.83	Almond Vegan	$0.20	$0.17
	Total Shipped	**21.26**	**Price per Dozen**	**$0.20**	**$4.25**

Shipping Report # 27623

Ordered	Date Shipped	Dozen Shipped	Description	Price per Dozen	Total
267	11/17/20X2	2.75	Carrot Cake	$0.20	$0.55
451	11/17/20X2	4.67	Chocolate	$0.20	$0.93
184	11/17/20X2	1.92	Gluten-free Choc.	$0.20	$0.38
328	11/17/20X2	3.42	Lemon	$0.20	$0.68
123	11/17/20X2	1.25	Red Velvet	$0.20	$0.25
164	11/17/20X2	1.75	Spice	$0.20	$0.35
451	11/17/20X2	4.67	Vanilla	$0.20	$0.93
82	11/17/20X2	0.83	Almond Vegan	$0.20	$0.17
	Total Shipped	**21.26**	**Price per Dozen**	**$0.20**	**$4.25**

Client Supporting Document

AR.4.3: pg. 6 of 12

SHIPPING INVOICE (continued)

Alpine Cupcakes, Inc.
1250 16th Street
Denver, Colorado 80202

Page 3/4

Shipped To:

Denver Bakery Café

321 17th Street

Denver, CO 80202

Ship Invoice Number: S6412

Date: 11/30/20X2

Shipping Report # 27662

Ordered		Date Shipped	Dozen Shipped	Description	Price per Dozen	Total
267	*AR.4.1*	11/21/20X2	2.75	Carrot Cake	$0.20	$0.55
451		11/21/20X2	4.67	Chocolate	$0.20	$0.93
184		11/21/20X2	1.92	Gluten-free Choc.	$0.20	$0.38
328		11/21/20X2	3.42	Lemon	$0.20	$0.68
123		11/21/20X2	1.25	Red Velvet	$0.20	$0.25
164		11/21/20X2	1.75	Spice	$0.20	$0.35
451		11/21/20X2	4.67	Vanilla	$0.20	$0.93
82		11/21/20X2	0.83	Almond Vegan	$0.20	$0.17
		Total Shipped	**21.26**	**Price per Dozen**	**$0.20**	**$4.25**

Shipping Report # 27698

Ordered	Date Shipped	Dozen Shipped	Description	Price per Dozen	Total
267	11/25/20X2	3.00	Carrot Cake	$0.20	$0.60
451	11/25/20X2	4.92	Chocolate	$0.20	$0.98
184	11/25/20X2	1.92	Gluten-free Choc.	$0.20	$0.38
328	11/25/20X2	3.42	Lemon	$0.20	$0.68
123	11/25/20X2	1.50	Red Velvet	$0.20	$0.30
164	11/25/20X2	1.42	Spice	$0.20	$0.28
451	11/25/20X2	4.92	Vanilla	$0.20	$0.98
82	11/25/20X2	1.00	Almond Vegan	$0.20	$0.20
	Total Shipped	**22.10**	**Price per Dozen**	**$0.20**	**$4.42**

Sales Tax	N/A
Invoice Total	$34.17

Please return this page with your payment

SHIPPING INVOICE

Remittance Advice

Denver Bakery Café
321 17th Street
Denver, CO 80202

Page 4/4

Invoice Number:	S6412
Sales Order No:	2735
Customer PO:	1117
Customer PO Date:	11/1/20X2
Total Due:	$34.17
Date Due:	12/30/20X2

Date Paid _____

Amount Paid _____

**Pmt Received
1/1/20X3**

Lindsay McKenna

See returned remittance form

Performed by:
TES 02/12/20X3
Reviewed by:
SDM 2/14/20x3

ALPINE CUPCAKES, INC.
Shipping Report

Date: 11/1/20X2 *AR.4.1*
Purchase Order #: 1117   **Shipping Report # 27398**
Shipped To: Denver Bakery Café
Freight Carrier: Alpine Cupcake Carrier

Quantity	Unit	Description
33	Cupcakes	Carrot Cake
56	Cupcakes	Chocolate
23	Cupcakes	Gluten-free Chocolate
41	Cupcakes	Lemon
15	Cupcakes	Red Velvet
21	Cupcakes	Spice
56	Cupcakes	Vanilla
10	Cupcakes	Almond Vegan

Remarks: *Items received in OK condition*
Received By: *Junior Yonk (Denver Bakery Receiving)*
Delivered To: *Receiving Dept.*

ALPINE CUPCAKES, INC.
Shipping Report

Date: 11/4/20X2 *AR.4.1*
Purchase Order #: 1117   **Shipping Report # 27482**
Shipped To: Denver Bakery Café
Freight Carrier: Alpine Cupcake Carrier

Quantity	Unit	Description
33	Cupcakes	Carrot Cake
56	Cupcakes	Chocolate
23	Cupcakes	Gluten-free Chocolate
41	Cupcakes	Lemon
15	Cupcakes	Red Velvet
21	Cupcakes	Spice
56	Cupcakes	Vanilla
10	Cupcakes	Almond Vegan

Remarks: *Items received in OK condition*
Received By: *Junior Yonk (Denver Bakery Receiving)*
Delivered To: *Receiving Dept.*

Alpine Cupcakes, Inc.
AR Aging Substantive Testing—Denver Bakery

Performed by:
TES 02/12/20X3
Reviewed by:
SDM 2/14/20X3

ALPINE CUPCAKES, INC.
Shipping Report

Date: 11/7/20X2   *AR.4.1*

Purchase Order #:   <u>1117</u>   **Shipping Report # 27501**

Shipped To: <u>Denver Bakery Café</u>

Freight Carrier: <u>Alpine Cupcake Carrier</u>

Quantity	Unit	Description
33	Cupcakes	Carrot Cake
56	Cupcakes	Chocolate
23	Cupcakes	Gluten-free Chocolate
41	Cupcakes	Lemon
15	Cupcakes	Red Velvet
21	Cupcakes	Spice
56	Cupcakes	Vanilla
10	Cupcakes	Almond Vegan

Remarks: *Items received in OK condition*

Received By: *Junior Yonk (Denver Bakery Receiving)*

Delivered To: *Receiving Dept.*

ALPINE CUPCAKES, INC.
Shipping Report

Date: 11/10/20X2   *AR.4.1*

Purchase Order #:   <u>1117</u>   **Shipping Report # 27578**

Shipped To: <u>Denver Bakery Café</u>

Freight Carrier: <u>Alpine Cupcake Carrier</u>

Quantity	Unit	Description
33	Cupcakes	Carrot Cake
56	Cupcakes	Chocolate
23	Cupcakes	Gluten-free Chocolate
41	Cupcakes	Lemon
15	Cupcakes	Red Velvet
21	Cupcakes	Spice
56	Cupcakes	Vanilla
10	Cupcakes	Almond Vegan

Remarks: *Items received in OK condition*

Received By: *Junior Yonk (Denver Bakery Receiving)*

Delivered To: *Receiving Dept.*

Client Supporting Document   AR.4.3: pg. 10 of 12

Performed by:
TES 02/12/20X3
Reviewed by:
SDM 2/14/20x3

ALPINE CUPCAKES, INC.
Shipping Report

Date: 11/14/20X2   *AR.4.1*

Purchase Order #:   1117   **Shipping Report # 27614**

Shipped To: Denver Bakery Café

Freight Carrier: Alpine Cupcake Carrier

Quantity	Unit	Description
33	Cupcakes	Carrot Cake
56	Cupcakes	Chocolate
23	Cupcakes	Gluten-free Chocolate
41	Cupcakes	Lemon
15	Cupcakes	Red Velvet
21	Cupcakes	Spice
56	Cupcakes	Vanilla
10	Cupcakes	Almond Vegan

Remarks: *Items received in OK condition*

Received By: *Junior Yonk (Denver Bakery Receiving)*

Delivered To: *Receiving Dept.*

ALPINE CUPCAKES, INC.
Shipping Report

Date: 11/17/20X2   *AR.4.1*

Purchase Order #:   1117   **Shipping Report # 27623**

Shipped To: Denver Bakery Café

Freight Carrier: Alpine Cupcake Carrier

Quantity	Unit	Description
33	Cupcakes	Carrot Cake
56	Cupcakes	Chocolate
23	Cupcakes	Gluten-free Chocolate
41	Cupcakes	Lemon
15	Cupcakes	Red Velvet
21	Cupcakes	Spice
56	Cupcakes	Vanilla
10	Cupcakes	Almond Vegan

Remarks: *Items in Poor condition—returned to Alpine*

Received By: *Junior Yonk (Denver Bakery Receiving)*

Delivered To: *Receiving Dept.*

Performed by:
TES 02/12/20X3
Reviewed by:
SDM 2/14/20x3

ALPINE CUPCAKES, INC.
Shipping Report

Date: 11/21/20X2 *AR.4.1*

Purchase Order #: 1117

Shipped To: Denver Bakery Café

Freight Carrier: Alpine Cupcake Carrier

Shipping Report # 27662

Quantity	Unit	Description
33	Cupcakes	Carrot Cake
56	Cupcakes	Chocolate
23	Cupcakes	Gluten-free Chocolate
41	Cupcakes	Lemon
15	Cupcakes	Red Velvet
21	Cupcakes	Spice
56	Cupcakes	Vanilla
10	Cupcakes	Almond Vegan

Remarks: *Items received in OK condition*

Received By: *Junior Yonk (Denver Bakery Receiving)*

Delivered To: *Receiving Dept.*

ALPINE CUPCAKES, INC.
Shipping Report

Date: 11/25/20X2 *AR.4.1*

Purchase Order #: 1117

Shipped To: Denver Bakery Café

Freight Carrier: Alpine Cupcake Carrier

Shipping Report # 27698

Quantity	Unit	Description
36	Cupcakes	Carrot Cake
59	Cupcakes	Chocolate
23	Cupcakes	Gluten-free Chocolate
41	Cupcakes	Lemon
18	Cupcakes	Red Velvet
17	Cupcakes	Spice
59	Cupcakes	Vanilla
12	Cupcakes	Almond Vegan

Remarks: *Items received in OK condition*

Received By: *Junior Yonk (Denver Bakery Receiving)*

Delivered To: *Receiving Dept.*

Client Supporting Document

AR.4.3: pg. 12 of 12

PRODUCT INVOICE

Alpine Cupcakes, Inc.
1250 16th Street
Denver, Colorado 80202

Page 1/4

Shipped To:
Luigi's Bistro
1500 Arapahoe Street
Denver, Colorado 80202
Customer PO: 896
Customer PO Date: 10/04/20X2

AR.4.1

Invoice Number: 6387
Date: 10/31/20X2
Due Date: 11/30/20X2
Sales Order No: 2710

No. Ordered	Date Shipped	No. Shipped	No. Left in Order	Description	Price	Total
55	10/5/20X2	7	48	Carrot Cake	$2.40	$16.80
100	10/5/20X2	13	87	Chocolate	$2.40	$31.20
25	10/5/20X2	3	22	Gluten-free Choc.	$2.40	$7.20
65	10/5/20X2	8	57	Lemon	$2.40	$19.20
50	10/5/20X2	6	44	Red Velvet	$2.40	$14.40
50	10/5/20X2	6	44	Spice	$2.40	$14.40
125	10/5/20X2	16	109	Vanilla	$2.40	$38.40
30	10/5/20X2	4	26	Almond Vegan	$2.40	$9.60
				Total Shipment		**$151.20**
55	10/8/20X2	7	41	Carrot Cake	$2.40	$16.80
100	10/8/20X2	13	74	Chocolate	$2.40	$31.20
25	10/8/20X2	3	19	Gluten-free Choc.	$2.40	$7.20
65	10/8/20X2	8	49	Lemon	$2.40	$19.20
50	10/8/20X2	6	38	Red Velvet	$2.40	$14.40
50	10/8/20X2	6	38	Spice	$2.40	$14.40
125	10/8/20X2	16	93	Vanilla	$2.40	$38.40
30	10/8/20X2	4	22	Almond Vegan	$2.40	$9.60
				Total Shipment		**$151.20**
55	10/12/20X2	7	34	Carrot Cake	$2.40	$16.80
100	10/12/20X2	13	61	Chocolate	$2.40	$31.20
25	10/12/20X2	3	16	Gluten-free Choc.	$2.40	$7.20
65	10/12/20X2	8	41	Lemon	$2.40	$19.20
50	10/12/20X2	6	32	Red Velvet	$2.40	$14.40
50	10/12/20X2	6	32	Spice	$2.40	$14.40
125	10/12/20X2	16	77	Vanilla	$2.40	$38.40
30	10/12/20X2	4	18	Almond Vegan	$2.40	$9.60
				Total Shipment		**$151.20**

Performed by:
TES 02/12/20X3
Reviewed by:
SDM 2/14/20x3

PRODUCT INVOICE

Alpine Cupcakes, Inc.
1250 16th Street
Denver, Colorado 80202

Page 2/4
Invoice Number: 6387
Date: 10/31/20X2

Shipped To:

Luigi's Bistro

1500 Arapahoe Street

Denver, Colorado 80202

Ordered	Date Shipped	No. Shipped	No. Left in Order	Description	Price	Total
55	10/15/20X2	7	27	Carrot Cake	$2.40	$16.80
100	10/15/20X2	13	48	Chocolate	$2.40	$31.20
25	10/15/20X2	3	13	Gluten-free Choc.	$2.40	$7.20
65	10/15/20X2	8	33	Lemon	$2.40	$19.20
50	10/15/20X2	6	26	Red Velvet	$2.40	$14.40
50	10/15/20X2	6	26	Spice	$2.40	$14.40
125	10/15/20X2	16	61	Vanilla	$2.40	$38.40
30	10/15/20X2	4	14	Almond Vegan	$2.40	$9.60
				Total Shipment		**$151.20**
55	10/19/20X2	7	20	Carrot Cake	$2.40	$16.80
100	10/19/20X2	13	35	Chocolate	$2.40	$31.20
25	10/19/20X2	3	10	Gluten-free Choc.	$2.40	$7.20
65	10/19/20X2	8	25	Lemon	$2.40	$19.20
50	10/19/20X2	6	20	Red Velvet	$2.40	$14.40
50	10/19/20X2	6	20	Spice	$2.40	$14.40
125	10/19/20X2	16	45	Vanilla	$2.40	$38.40
30	10/19/20X2	4	10	Almond Vegan	$2.40	$9.60
				Total Shipment		**$151.20**
55	10/23/20X2	7	13	Carrot Cake	$2.40	$16.80
100	10/23/20X2	13	22	Chocolate	$2.40	$31.20
25	10/23/20X2	3	7	Gluten-free Choc.	$2.40	$7.20
65	10/23/20X2	8	17	Lemon	$2.40	$19.20
50	10/23/20X2	6	14	Red Velvet	$2.40	$14.40
50	10/23/20X2	6	14	Spice	$2.40	$14.40
125	10/23/20X2	16	29	Vanilla	$2.40	$38.40
30	10/23/20X2	4	6	Almond Vegan	$2.40	$9.60
				Total Shipment		**$151.20**

Client Supporting Document

AR.4.4: pg. 2 of 8

Performed by:
TES 02/12/20X3
Reviewed by:
SDM 2/14/20x3

PRODUCT INVOICE

Alpine Cupcakes, Inc.
1250 16th Street
Denver, Colorado 80202

Page 3/4

Invoice Number: 6387

Date: 10/31/20X2

Shipped To:

Luigi's Bistro

1500 Arapahoe Street

Denver, Colorado 80202

Ordered	Date Shipped	No. Shipped	No. Left in Order	Description	Price	Total
55	10/26/20X2	7	6	Carrot Cake	$2.40	$16.80
100	10/26/20X2	13	9	Chocolate	$2.40	$31.20
25	10/26/20X2	3	4	Gluten-free Choc.	$2.40	$7.20
65	10/26/20X2	8	9	Lemon	$2.40	$19.20
50	10/26/20X2	6	8	Red Velvet	$2.40	$14.40
50	10/26/20X2	6	8	Spice	$2.40	$14.40
125	10/26/20X2	16	13	Vanilla	$2.40	$38.40
30	10/26/20X2	4	2	Almond Vegan	$2.40	$9.60
				Total Shipment		**$151.20**
55	10/29/20X2	6	0	Carrot Cake	$2.40	$14.40
100	10/29/20X2	9	0	Chocolate	$2.40	$21.60
25	10/29/20X2	4	0	Gluten-free Choc.	$2.40	$9.60
65	10/29/20X2	9	0	Lemon	$2.40	$21.60
50	10/29/20X2	8	0	Red Velvet	$2.40	$19.20
50	10/29/20X2	8	0	Spice	$2.40	$19.20
125	10/29/20X2	13	0	Vanilla	$2.40	$31.20
30	10/29/20X2	2	0	Almond Vegan	$2.40	$4.80
				Total Shipment		**$141.60**

Sales Tax	N/A
Freight	N/A
Invoice Total	$1,200.00

Performed by:
TES 02/12/20X3
Reviewed by:
SDM 2/14/20x3

Please return this page with your payment

PRODUCT INVOICE

Page 4/4

Remittance Advice

Luigi's Bistro
1500 Arapahoe Street
Denver, Colorado 80202

Invoice Number:	6387
Sales Order No:	2710
Customer PO:	896
Customer PO Date:	10/4/20X2
Total Amount Owed:	$1,200.00
Date due:	11/30/X2

Date Paid _____

Amount Paid _____

Pmt Received

1/3/20X3

Lindsay McKenna

See returned remittance form

Performed by:
TES 02/12/20X3
Reviewed by:
SDM 2/14/20x3

ALPINE CUPCAKES, INC.
Shipping Report

Date: 10/5/20X2 *AR.4.1*

Purchase Order #: 896

Shipped To: Luigi's Bistro

Freight Carrier: Alpine Cupcake Carrier

Shipping Report # 27050

Quantity	Unit	Description
7	Cupcakes	Carrot Cake
13	Cupcakes	Chocolate
3	Cupcakes	Gluten-free Chocolate
8	Cupcakes	Lemon
6	Cupcakes	Red Velvet
6	Cupcakes	Spice
16	Cupcakes	Vanilla
4	Cupcakes	Almond Vegan

Remarks: *Items received in good condition*

Received By: *Kaitlynn Morgan (Luigi Receiving)*

Delivered To: *Receiving Dept.*

ALPINE CUPCAKES, INC.
Shipping Report

Date: 10/8/20X2 *AR.4.1*

Purchase Order #: 896

Shipped To: Luigi's Bistro

Freight Carrier: Alpine Cupcake Carrier

Shipping Report # 27120

Quantity	Unit	Description
7	Cupcakes	Carrot Cake
13	Cupcakes	Chocolate
3	Cupcakes	Gluten-free Chocolate
8	Cupcakes	Lemon
6	Cupcakes	Red Velvet
6	Cupcakes	Spice
16	Cupcakes	Vanilla
4	Cupcakes	Almond Vegan

Remarks: *Items received in good condition*

Received By: *Kaitlynn Morgan (Luigi Receiving)*

Delivered To: *Receiving Dept.*

Client Supporting Document

AR.4.4: pg. 5 of 8

Performed by:
TES 02/12/20X3
Reviewed by:
SDM 2/14/20x3

ALPINE CUPCAKES, INC.
Shipping Report

Date:	10/12/20X2 *AR.4.1*	
Purchase Order #:	896	**Shipping Report # 27155**
Shipped To:	Luigi's Bistro	
Freight Carrier:	Alpine Cupcake Carrier	

Quantity	Unit	Description
7	Cupcakes	Carrot Cake
13	Cupcakes	Chocolate
3	Cupcakes	Gluten-free Chocolate
8	Cupcakes	Lemon
6	Cupcakes	Red Velvet
6	Cupcakes	Spice
16	Cupcakes	Vanilla
4	Cupcakes	Almond Vegan

Remarks: *Items received in good condition*

Received By: *Kaitlynn Morgan (Luigi Receiving)*

Delivered To: *Receiving Dept.*

ALPINE CUPCAKES, INC.
Shipping Report

Date:	10/15/20X2 *AR.4.1*	
Purchase Order #:	896	**Shipping Report # 27175**
Shipped To:	Luigi's Bistro	
Freight Carrier:	Alpine Cupcake Carrier	

Quantity	Unit	Description
7	Cupcakes	Carrot Cake
13	Cupcakes	Chocolate
3	Cupcakes	Gluten-free Chocolate
8	Cupcakes	Lemon
6	Cupcakes	Red Velvet
6	Cupcakes	Spice
16	Cupcakes	Vanilla
4	Cupcakes	Almond Vegan

Remarks: *Items received in good condition*

Received By: *Kaitlynn Morgan (Luigi Receiving)*

Delivered To: *Receiving Dept.*

Client Supporting Document

AR.4.4: pg. 6 of 8

Performed by:
TES 02/12/20X3
Reviewed by:
SDM 2/14/20x3

ALPINE CUPCAKES, INC.
Shipping Report

Date: 10/19/20X2 *AR.4.1*

Purchase Order #: 896   **Shipping Report # 27207**

Shipped To: Luigi's Bistro

Freight Carrier: Alpine Cupcake Carrier

Quantity	Unit	Description
7	Cupcakes	Carrot Cake
13	Cupcakes	Chocolate
3	Cupcakes	Gluten-free Chocolate
8	Cupcakes	Lemon
6	Cupcakes	Red Velvet
6	Cupcakes	Spice
16	Cupcakes	Vanilla
4	Cupcakes	Almond Vegan

Remarks: *Items received in good condition*

Received By: *Kaitlynn Morgan (Luigi Receiving)*

Delivered To: *Receiving Dept.*

ALPINE CUPCAKES, INC.
Shipping Report

Date: 10/23/20X2 *AR.4.1*

Purchase Order #: 896   **Shipping Report # 27222**

Shipped To: Luigi's Bistro

Freight Carrier: Alpine Cupcake Carrier

Quantity	Unit	Description
7	Cupcakes	Carrot Cake
13	Cupcakes	Chocolate
3	Cupcakes	Gluten-free Chocolate
8	Cupcakes	Lemon
6	Cupcakes	Red Velvet
6	Cupcakes	Spice
16	Cupcakes	Vanilla
4	Cupcakes	Almond Vegan

Remarks: *Items received in good condition*

Received By: *Kaitlynn Morgan (Luigi Receiving)*

Delivered To: *Receiving Dept.*

Client Supporting Document   AR.4.4: pg. 7 of 8

Performed by:
TES 02/12/20X3
Reviewed by:
SDM 2/14/20x3

ALPINE CUPCAKES, INC.
Shipping Report

Date: 10/26/20X2   *AR.4.1*

Purchase Order #: 896

Shipping Report # 27284

Shipped To: Luigi's Bistro

Freight Carrier: Alpine Cupcake Carrier

Quantity	Unit	Description
7	Cupcakes	Carrot Cake
13	Cupcakes	Chocolate
3	Cupcakes	Gluten-free Chocolate
8	Cupcakes	Lemon
6	Cupcakes	Red Velvet
6	Cupcakes	Spice
16	Cupcakes	Vanilla
4	Cupcakes	Almond Vegan

Remarks: *Items received*

Received By: *Lindsay McKenna*

Delivered To: *AR Dept.*

ALPINE CUPCAKES, INC.
Shipping Report

Date: 10/29/20X2   *AR.4.1*

Purchase Order #: 896

Shipping Report # 27337

Shipped To: Luigi's Bistro

Freight Carrier: Alpine Cupcake Carrier

Quantity	Unit	Description
6	Cupcakes	Carrot Cake
9	Cupcakes	Chocolate
4	Cupcakes	Gluten-free Chocolate
9	Cupcakes	Lemon
8	Cupcakes	Red Velvet
8	Cupcakes	Spice
13	Cupcakes	Vanilla
2	Cupcakes	Almond Vegan

Remarks: *Items received*

Received By: *Lindsay McKenna*

Delivered To: *AR Dept.*

Performed by:
TES 02/12/20X3
Reviewed by:
SDM 2/14/20x3

PRODUCT INVOICE

Alpine Cupcakes, Inc.
1250 16th Street
Denver, Colorado 80202

Page 1/4

Shipped To:

Invoice Number: 6343

Buckhead Restaurants
2700 Welton Street
Denver, Colorado 80205

AR.4.1   Date: 9/30/20X2

Due Date: 10/30/20X2

Customer PO Date: 09/02/20X2   Customer PO: 1720   Sales Order No: 2666

No. Ordered	Date Shipped	No. Shipped	No. Left in Order	Description	Price	Total
93	9/3/20X2	12	81	Carrot Cake	$2.40	$28.80
162	9/3/20X2	20	142	Chocolate	$2.40	$48.00
54	9/3/20X2	7	47	Gluten-free Choc.	$2.40	$16.80
108	9/3/20X2	14	94	Lemon	$2.40	$33.60
62	9/3/20X2	8	54	Red Velvet	$2.40	$19.20
69	9/3/20X2	9	60	Spice	$2.40	$21.60
186	9/3/20X2	23	163	Vanilla	$2.40	$55.20
38	9/3/20X2	5	33	Almond Vegan	$2.40	$12.00
				Total Shipment		**$235.20**
93	9/7/20X2	12	69	Carrot Cake	$2.40	$28.80
162	9/7/20X2	20	122	Chocolate	$2.40	$48.00
54	9/7/20X2	7	40	Gluten-free Choc.	$2.40	$16.80
108	9/7/20X2	14	80	Lemon	$2.40	$33.60
62	9/7/20X2	8	46	Red Velvet	$2.40	$19.20
69	9/7/20X2	9	51	Spice	$2.40	$21.60
186	9/7/20X2	23	140	Vanilla	$2.40	$55.20
38	9/7/20X2	5	28	Almond Vegan	$2.40	$12.00
				Total Shipment		**$235.20**
93	9/10/20X2	12	57	Carrot Cake	$2.40	$28.80
162	9/10/20X2	20	102	Chocolate	$2.40	$48.00
54	9/10/20X2	7	33	Gluten-free Choc.	$2.40	$16.80
108	9/10/20X2	14	66	Lemon	$2.40	$33.60
62	9/10/20X2	8	38	Red Velvet	$2.40	$19.20
69	9/10/20X2	9	42	Spice	$2.40	$21.60
186	9/10/20X2	23	117	Vanilla	$2.40	$55.20
38	9/10/20X2	5	23	Almond Vegan	$2.40	$12.00
				Total Shipment		**$235.20**

PRODUCT INVOICE

Alpine Cupcakes, Inc.
1250 16th Street
Denver, Colorado 80202

Page 2/4

Shipped To:

Invoice Number: 6343

Buckhead Restaurants

Date: 9/30/20X2

2700 Welton Street

Denver, Colorado 80205

Ordered	Date Shipped	No. Shipped	No. Left in Order	Description	Price	Total
93	9/14/20X2	12	45	Carrot Cake	$2.40	$28.80
162	9/14/20X2	20	82	Chocolate	$2.40	$48.00
54	9/14/20X2	7	26	Gluten-free Choc.	$2.40	$16.80
108	9/14/20X2	14	52	Lemon	$2.40	$33.60
62	9/14/20X2	8	30	Red Velvet	$2.40	$19.20
69	9/14/20X2	9	33	Spice	$2.40	$21.60
186	9/14/20X2	23	94	Vanilla	$2.40	$55.20
38	9/14/20X2	5	18	Almond Vegan	$2.40	$12.00
				Total Shipment		**$235.20**
93	9/21/20X2	12	33	Carrot Cake	$2.40	$28.80
162	9/21/20X2	20	62	Chocolate	$2.40	$48.00
54	9/21/20X2	7	19	Gluten-free Choc.	$2.40	$16.80
108	9/21/20X2	14	38	Lemon	$2.40	$33.60
62	9/21/20X2	8	22	Red Velvet	$2.40	$19.20
69	9/21/20X2	9	24	Spice	$2.40	$21.60
186	9/21/20X2	23	71	Vanilla	$2.40	$55.20
38	9/21/20X2	5	13	Almond Vegan	$2.40	$12.00
				Total Shipment		**$235.20**
93	9/23/20X2	12	21	Carrot Cake	$2.40	$28.80
162	9/23/20X2	20	42	Chocolate	$2.40	$48.00
54	9/23/20X2	7	12	Gluten-free Choc.	$2.40	$16.80
108	9/23/20X2	14	24	Lemon	$2.40	$33.60
62	9/23/20X2	8	14	Red Velvet	$2.40	$19.20
69	9/23/20X2	9	15	Spice	$2.40	$21.60
186	9/23/20X2	23	48	Vanilla	$2.40	$55.20
38	9/23/20X2	5	8	Almond Vegan	$2.40	$12.00
				Total Shipment		**$235.20**

PRODUCT INVOICE

Alpine Cupcakes, Inc.
1250 16th Street
Denver, Colorado 80202

Page 3/4

Shipped To:

Buckhead Restaurants

2700 Welton Street

Denver, Colorado 80205

Invoice Number: 6343

Date: 9/30/20x2

Ordered	Date Shipped	No. Shipped	No. Left in Order	Description	Price	Total
93	9/27/20X2	12	9	Carrot Cake	$2.40	$28.80
162	9/27/20X2	20	22	Chocolate	$2.40	$48.00
54	9/27/20X2	7	5	Gluten-free Choc.	$2.40	$16.80
108	9/27/20X2	14	10	Lemon	$2.40	$33.60
62	9/27/20X2	8	6	Red Velvet	$2.40	$19.20
69	9/27/20X2	9	6	Spice	$2.40	$21.60
186	9/27/20X2	23	25	Vanilla	$2.40	$55.20
38	9/27/20X2	5	3	Almond Vegan	$2.40	$12.00
				Total Shipment		**$235.20**
93	9/30/20X2	9	0	Carrot Cake	$2.40	$21.60
162	9/30/20X2	22	0	Chocolate	$2.40	$52.80
54	9/30/20X2	5	0	Gluten-free Choc.	$2.40	$12.00
108	9/30/20X2	10	0	Lemon	$2.40	$24.00
62	9/30/20X2	6	0	Red Velvet	$2.40	$14.40
69	9/30/20X2	6	0	Spice	$2.40	$14.40
186	9/30/20X2	25	0	Vanilla	$2.40	$60.00
38	9/30/20X2	3	0	Almond Vegan	$2.40	$7.20
				Total Shipment		**$206.40**

Sales Tax	N/A
Freight	N/A
Invoice Total	$1,852.80

Please return this page with your payment

PRODUCT INVOICE

Remittance Advice

Buckhead Restaurants
2700 Welton Street
Denver, Colorado 80205

Page 4/4

Invoice Number:	6343
Sales Order No:	2666
Customer PO:	1720
Customer PO Date:	9/02/20X2
Total amount Owed:	$1,852.80
Date due:	10/30/X2

Date Paid _____

Amount Paid _____

Pmt Received

1/11/20X3

Lindsay McKenna

See returned remittance form

Performed by:
TES 02/12/20X3
Reviewed by:
SDM 2/14/20X3

ALPINE CUPCAKES, INC.
Shipping Report

Date: 9/3/20X2 *AR.4.1*

Purchase Order #:   1720   **Shipping Report # 27050**

Shipped To: Buckhead Restaurants

Freight Carrier: Alpine Cupcake Carrier

Quantity	Unit	Description
12	Cupcakes	Carrot Cake
20	Cupcakes	Chocolate
7	Cupcakes	Gluten-free Chocolate
14	Cupcakes	Lemon
8	Cupcakes	Red Velvet
9	Cupcakes	Spice
23	Cupcakes	Vanilla
5	Cupcakes	Almond Vegan

Remarks: *Items received in good condition*

Received By: *Lindsay Jorgensen (Buckhead Receiving)*

Delivered To: *Receiving Dept.*

ALPINE CUPCAKES, INC.
Shipping Report

Date: 9/7/20X2 *AR.4.1*

Purchase Order #:   1720   **Shipping Report # 27120**

Shipped To: Buckhead Restaurants

Freight Carrier: Alpine Cupcake Carrier

Quantity	Unit	Description
12	Cupcakes	Carrot Cake
20	Cupcakes	Chocolate
7	Cupcakes	Gluten-free Chocolate
14	Cupcakes	Lemon
8	Cupcakes	Red Velvet
9	Cupcakes	Spice
23	Cupcakes	Vanilla
5	Cupcakes	Almond Vegan

Remarks: *Items received in good condition*

Received By: *Lindsay Jorgensen (Buckhead Receiving)*

Delivered To: *Receiving Dept.*

Client Supporting Document

AR.4.5: pg. 5 of 8

Performed by:
TES 02/12/20X3
Reviewed by:
SDM 2/14/20x3

ALPINE CUPCAKES, INC.
Shipping Report

Date:	9/10/20X2 *AR.4.1*	
Purchase Order #:	1720	**Shipping Report # 27155**
Shipped To:	Buckhead Restaurants	
Freight Carrier:	Alpine Cupcake Carrier	

Quantity	Unit	Description
12	Cupcakes	Carrot Cake
20	Cupcakes	Chocolate
7	Cupcakes	Gluten-free Chocolate
14	Cupcakes	Lemon
8	Cupcakes	Red Velvet
9	Cupcakes	Spice
23	Cupcakes	Vanilla
5	Cupcakes	Almond Vegan

Remarks: *Items received in good condition*

Received By: *Lindsay Jorgensen (Buckhead Receiving)*

Delivered To: *Receiving Dept.*

ALPINE CUPCAKES, INC.
Shipping Report

Date:	9/14/20X2 *AR.4.1*	
Purchase Order #:	1720	**Shipping Report # 27175**
Shipped To:	Buckhead Restaurants	
Freight Carrier:	Alpine Cupcake Carrier	

Quantity	Unit	Description
12	Cupcakes	Carrot Cake
20	Cupcakes	Chocolate
7	Cupcakes	Gluten-free Chocolate
14	Cupcakes	Lemon
8	Cupcakes	Red Velvet
9	Cupcakes	Spice
23	Cupcakes	Vanilla
5	Cupcakes	Almond Vegan

Remarks: *Items received in good condition*

Received By: *Lindsay Jorgensen (Buckhead Receiving)*

Delivered To: *Receiving Dept.*

Client Supporting Document

AR.4.5: pg. 6 of 8

Performed by:
TES 02/12/20X3
Reviewed by:
SDM 2/14/20X3

ALPINE CUPCAKES, INC.
Shipping Report

Date: 9/21/20X2   *AR.4.1*

Purchase Order #:   1720   **Shipping Report # 27207**

Shipped To: Buckhead Restaurants

Freight Carrier: Alpine Cupcake Carrier

Quantity	Unit	Description
12	Cupcakes	Carrot Cake
20	Cupcakes	Chocolate
7	Cupcakes	Gluten-free Chocolate
14	Cupcakes	Lemon
8	Cupcakes	Red Velvet
9	Cupcakes	Spice
23	Cupcakes	Vanilla
5	Cupcakes	Almond Vegan

Remarks: *Items received in good condition*

Received By: *Lindsay Jorgensen (Buckhead Receiving)*

Delivered To: *Receiving Dept.*

ALPINE CUPCAKES, INC.
Shipping Report

Date: 9/23/20X2   *AR.4.1*

Purchase Order #:   1720   **Shipping Report # 27222**

Shipped To: Buckhead Restaurants

Freight Carrier: Alpine Cupcake Carrier

Quantity	Unit	Description
12	Cupcakes	Carrot Cake
20	Cupcakes	Chocolate
7	Cupcakes	Gluten-free Chocolate
14	Cupcakes	Lemon
8	Cupcakes	Red Velvet
9	Cupcakes	Spice
23	Cupcakes	Vanilla
5	Cupcakes	Almond Vegan

Remarks: *Items received in good condition*

Received By: *Lindsay Jorgensen (Buckhead Receiving)*

Delivered To: *Receiving Dept.*

Client Supporting Document

AR.4.5: pg. 7 of 8

ALPINE CUPCAKES, INC.
Shipping Report

Date: 9/27/20X2 *AR.4.1*

Purchase Order #:   1720   **Shipping Report # 27284**

Shipped To: Buckhead Restaurants

Freight Carrier: Alpine Cupcake Carrier

Quantity	Unit	Description
12	Cupcakes	Carrot Cake
20	Cupcakes	Chocolate
7	Cupcakes	Gluten-free Chocolate
14	Cupcakes	Lemon
8	Cupcakes	Red Velvet
9	Cupcakes	Spice
23	Cupcakes	Vanilla
5	Cupcakes	Almond Vegan

Remarks: *Items received in good condition*

Received By: *Lindsay Jorgensen (Buckhead Receiving)*

Delivered To: *Receiving Dept.*

ALPINE CUPCAKES, INC.
Shipping Report

Date: 10/02/20X2 *AR.4.1*

Purchase Order #:   1720   **Shipping Report # 27337**

Shipped To: Buckhead Restaurants

Freight Carrier: Alpine Cupcake Carrier

Quantity	Unit	Description
9	Cupcakes	Carrot Cake
22	Cupcakes	Chocolate
5	Cupcakes	Gluten-free Chocolate
10	Cupcakes	Lemon
6	Cupcakes	Red Velvet
6	Cupcakes	Spice
25	Cupcakes	Vanilla
3	Cupcakes	Almond Vegan

Remarks: *Items received in good condition*

Received By: *Lindsay Jorgensen (Buckhead Receiving)*

Delivered To: *Receiving Dept.*

Client Supporting Document   AR.4.5: pg. 8 of 8

Alpine Cupcakes, Inc.
AR Confirmation Memo and Log
Audit Year December 31, 20X2

Garcia and Foster, CPAs, LLC

Performed by: TES
Date: 02/01/2013

Reviewed by: SDM
Date: 2/7/20X3

We selected the 5 largest AR balances as of 12/31/20X2 for the AR Confirmation letters. Per AR.4.2, the 5 largest accounts are as follows

Customer Name	12/31/20X2 AR Balance
Mile High Steakhouses	$20,550.57
Bon Appetito Restaurants	$17,085.83
UC Boulder Food Service	$14,761.00
The Sandwich Place	$12,432.20
Buckhead Restaurants	$12,147.95

We requested that Alexis Madison prepare and sign the AR confirmations. Alexis prepared the confirmations by filling in the client information, including the client's name, address, contact, and the AR balance as of 12/31/20X2. Then Alexis reviewed the forms and signed the documents. Alexis gave us the confirmations. We reviewed the confirmations and put the letters in Alpine's outgoing mail bin in the Company's mailroom. Before mailing the confirmations, we included a self-addressed envelope to be sent with the confirmation letters. Mile High Steakhouses, UC Boulder Food Service, The Sandwich Place, and Buckhead Restaurants all mailed their confirmations back to our office. Bon Appetito Restaurants mailed the letter back to Alpine Cupcakes. The letter was unopened and Alexis told us that the letter had just come in the mail and gave it directly to us. We determined that the letter was unopened and we did not have to send another confirmation.

Number	Customer Name	Date Sent	Second Request Sent (date)	Date Confirmation Received	Balance per AR Subledger	Amount Confirmed	Difference	Explanation of Differences
1	Mile High Steakhouses	1/05/20X3		1/12/20X3	$20,550.57	$11,392.17	$9,158.40	Payment of $9,158.40 in transit.
2	Bon Appetito Restaurants	1/05/20X3		1/14/20X3	$17,085.83	$17,085.83	$0.00	
3	UC Boulder Food Service	1/05/20X3		1/9/20X3	$14,761.00	$14,761.00	$0.00	
4	Buckhead Restaurants	1/05/20X3	1/15/20X3	1/20/20X3	$12,147.95	$0.00	$12,147.95	There is a dispute about the payments.
5	The Sandwich Place	1/05/20X6		1/12/20X3	$12,432.20	$0.00	$12,432.20	Payment made on 12/30/20X2 for $1,591.20.

Garcia and Foster Audit Workpaper

AR.5.1: pg. 1 of 1

Performed by:
TES 02/01/20X3
Reviewed by:
SDM 2/7/20x3

1/05/20X3

Mile High Steak House
1730 19th Street
Denver, CO 80202

Dear Madam:

Please confirm directly to our auditors, Garcia and Foster CPA, LLC, 1790 Lawrence Street, Denver, CO 80202 the correctness of the balance of your account payable to us as of December 31st, 20X2. The amount is listed below on the enclosed statement. If you do not agree with the amount, please provide additional information to aid our auditors in reconciling the difference.

Your prompt return of the form is appreciated and essential to the completion of our audit. Please note that this is not a request for payment. We are only requesting confirmation of your account balance.

Sincerely,
Alpine Cupcakes, Inc.

Signed By: _Alexis Madison_

--| AR.4.2 |--

The statement of our account showing a balance of $20,550.57 payable to Alpine Cupcakes, Inc. at December 31, 20X2, is correct except as noted below.

Mile High Steak House

Date _____01/10/20X3_____   By_____Lindsay Jones_____

Exceptions: _This differs from our books, which show that we paid $9,158.40 on 12/31/20X2. The invoices for product of $11,313.60 and shipping of $78.57 were still outstanding at the end of the year._

Auditor Notes:

I tied the $9,158.40 to the client's January mailroom control listing (AR.5.7) and to the general ledger entry (AR.5.8). Since the cash was not received until after year end, the ending AR balance of $20,550.57 appears appropriate.

Garcia and Foster Audit Workpaper

Performed by:
TES 02/01/20X3
Reviewed by:
SDM 2/7/20x3

1/05/20X3

Bon Appetito Restaurants
5011 Washington
Denver, CO 80113

**RECEIVED BY
ALPINE
CUPCAKES, INC.
JAN 14 20X3**

Dear Sir:

Please confirm directly to our auditors, Garcia and Foster CPA, LLC, 1790 Lawrence Street, Denver, CO 80202 the correctness of the balance of your account payable to us as of December 31st, 20X2. The amount is listed below on the enclosed statement. If you do not agree with the amount, please provide additional information to aid our auditors in reconciling the difference.

Your prompt return of the form is appreciated and essential to the completion of our audit. Please note that this is not a request for payment. We are only requesting confirmation of your account balance.

Sincerely,
Alpine Cupcakes, Inc.

Signed By: *Alexis Madison*

--- *AR.4.2* ---

The statement of our account showing a balance of $17,085.83 payable to Alpine Cupcakes, Inc. at December 31, 20X2, is correct except as noted below.

Bon Appetito Restaurants

Date ____*01/13/20X3*____   By_____*Jesse Kilborn*_____

Exceptions: *No exceptions. The total includes 2 invoices. A product invoice of $16,968.00 and a shipping invoice of $117.83, both due 1/30/20X3.*

Auditor Notes:

The ending AR balance of $17,085.83 appears appropriate.

1/05/20X3

UC Boulder Food Service
PO Box 5432
Aurora, CO 80012

Dear Madam:

Please confirm directly to our auditors, Garcia and Foster CPA, LLC, 1790 Lawrence Street, Denver, CO 80202 the correctness of the balance of your account payable to us as of December 31st, 20X2. The amount is listed below on the enclosed statement. If you do not agree with the amount, please provide additional information to aid our auditors in reconciling the difference.

Your prompt return of the form is appreciated and essential to the completion of our audit. Please note that this is not a request for payment. We are only requesting confirmation of your account balance.

Sincerely,
Alpine Cupcakes, Inc.

Signed By: *Alexis Madison*

---| *AR.4.2* |--

The statement of our account showing a balance of $14,761.00 payable to Alpine Cupcakes, Inc. at December 31, 20X2, is correct except as noted below.

UC Boulder Food Service

Date ___01/07/20X3___   By_____*Denise Bybee*_____

Exceptions: *No exceptions.*

Auditor Notes:

The ending AR balance of $14,761.00 appears appropriate.

Performed by:
TES 02/01/20X3
Reviewed by:
SDM 2/7/20X3

1/05/20X3

Buckhead Restaurants
2700 Welton Street
Denver, CO 80205

Dear Sir:

Please confirm directly to our auditors, Garcia and Foster CPA, LLC, 1790 Lawrence Street, Denver, CO 80202 the correctness of the balance of your account payable to us as of December 31st, 20X2. The amount is listed below on the enclosed statement. If you do not agree with the amount, please provide additional information to aid our auditors in reconciling the difference.

Your prompt return of the form is appreciated and essential to the completion of our audit. Please note that this is not a request for payment. We are only requesting confirmation of your account balance.

Sincerely,
Alpine Cupcakes, Inc.

Signed By: *Alexis Madison*

-- AR.4.2 --

The statement of our account showing a balance of $12,147.95 payable to Alpine Cupcakes, Inc. at December 31, 20X2, is correct except as noted below.

Buckhead Restaurants

Date ___*01/18/20X3*___   By ___*Chad Larsen*___

Exceptions: *Due to the quality of the goods received, we believe that we do not owe for the cupcakes delivered on September, October, and November 20X2. We have asked for a credit in the amount of $9,487.20*

Auditor Notes:

Per discussion with Alexis Madison, Buckhead Restaurants received the goods and owes Alpine Cupcakes the full amount. The client has already paid the shipping invoices related to these transactions. Alexis believes that Buckhead has some cash flow issues and will pay the amount in the next few months. Alexis says that she will meet with the customer in February to resolve the issue. Alexis assures us that she will have the full amount paid to Alpine. The AR Balance appears appropriate.

Garcia and Foster Audit Workpaper   AR.5.5: pg. 1 of 1

1/05/20X3

The Sandwich Place
1741 Broadway
Denver, CO 80274

Dear Madam:

Please confirm directly to our auditors, Garcia and Foster CPA, LLC, 1790 Lawrence Street, Denver, CO 80202 the correctness of the balance of your account payable to us as of December 31st, 20X2. The amount is listed below on the enclosed statement. If you do not agree with the amount, please provide additional information to aid our auditors in reconciling the difference.

Your prompt return of the form is appreciated and essential to the completion of our audit. Please note that this is not a request for payment. We are only requesting confirmation of your account balance.

Sincerely,
Alpine Cupcakes, Inc.

Signed By: *Alexis Madison*

--- | AR.4.2 | ---

The statement of our account showing a balance of $2,432.20 payable to Alpine Cupcakes, Inc. at December 31, 20X2, is correct except as noted below.

The Sandwich Place

Date ___01/9/20X3_____   By____Lorene Madison_____

Exceptions: *As of 12/31/20X2, we owed only $841.00. We paid $1,591.20 on 12/20/20X2.*

Auditor Notes:

I tied the $1,591.20 to the client's January mailroom control listing (AR.5.7) and to the general ledger entry (AR.5.8). The cash was received on 1/2/20X3. Since the cash was not received until after year end, the ending AR balance of $2,432.20 appears appropriate.

Performed by:
TES 02/01/20X3
Reviewed by:
SDM 2/7/20x3

PBC

Created By: ___*Diana Hayes*___ Date: ___*Daily Entries*___

Reviewed By: ___*Miguel Lopez*___ Date: ___*2/4/20X3*___

Item No.	Date	Customer Name	Customer Number	Amount	
1	1/1/20X3	Denver Bakery Café	99242	$34.17	
2	1/1/20X3	High Country Coffee	68752	$45.60	
3	1/2/20X3	Brown's Tavern	31965	$240.00	
4	1/2/20X3	Denver Bakery Café	99242	$4,920.00	
5	1/2/20X3	Denver Sirloin Restaurants	52058	$3,535.20	
6	1/2/20X3	Little's Grill	18860	$940.80	
7	1/2/20X3	Mile High Steakhouses	66286	$9,158.40	AR.5.2
8	1/2/20X3	Pebbles Inn	75763	$446.40	
9	1/2/20X3	Scotty's Taverns	43075	$369.60	
10	1/2/20X3	Smokey's Barbeque Pit	86485	$4,183.20	
11	1/2/20X3	Steinberg Delis	51535	$1,754.40	
12	1/2/20X3	The Sandwich Place	72927	$1,591.20	AR.5.6
13	1/3/20X3	Luigi's Bistro	43288	$1,200.00	
14	1/11/20X3	Buckhead Restaurants	13438	$1,852.80	
15	1/25/20X3	Broken Eggs Restaurant	62950	$15.02	
16	1/25/20X3	Bubba's Fish House	53277	$8.47	
17	1/25/20X3	Mountain Lion Restaurant	12295	$23.45	
18	1/25/20X3	Mountain Trout Fish House	72609	$3,434.40	
19	1/25/20X3	Papa's Restaurant	30700	$3,194.40	
20	1/25/20X3	UC Boulder Food Service	89500	$101.80	
21	1/25/20X3	UC Denver Food Service	40669	$11,368.80	
22	1/26/20X3	Buckhead Restaurants	13438	$18.35	
23	1/26/20X3	Julie's Wraps	59316	$11.18	
24	1/26/20X3	Little's Grill	18860	$1,132.80	
25	1/26/20X3	Pebbles Inn	75763	$10.92	
26	1/26/20X3	St. Francis Hotel and Spa	46367	$38.92	

Client Supporting Document

AR.5.7: pg. 1 of 3

Performed by:
TES 02/01/20X3
Reviewed by:
SDM 2/7/20X3

Item No.	Date	Customer Name	Customer Number	Amount
27	1/26/20X3	Steinberg Delis	51535	$14.52
28	1/26/20X3	The Sandwich Place	72927	$5.80
29	1/26/20X3	The Sandwich Place	72927	$835.20
30	1/27/20X3	Chavez Cantina	73678	$32.78
31	1/27/20X3	Country Barrel Restaurants	27978	$8,452.80
32	1/27/20X3	Granny's Café	40435	$26.00
33	1/27/20X3	Nora's Café	67694	$30.85
34	1/27/20X3	Scotty's Taverns	43075	$15.78
35	1/27/20X3	Steinberg Delis	51535	$2,090.40
36	1/28/20X3	Bon Appetito Restaurants	43754	$117.83
37	1/28/20X3	Boulder Tea House	58300	$578.40
38	1/28/20X3	Brown's Tavern	31965	$3.12
39	1/28/20X3	Bubba's Fish House	53277	$1,219.20
40	1/28/20X3	Denver Bakery Café	99242	$5,791.20
41	1/28/20X3	Denver Sirloin Restaurants	52058	$32.40
42	1/28/20X3	Fontana Catering & Café	33692	$23.85
43	1/29/20X3	Broken Eggs Restaurant	62950	$2,162.40
44	1/29/20X3	Country Barrel Restaurants	27978	$58.70
45	1/29/20X3	Denver Bakery Café	99242	$40.22
46	1/29/20X3	Denver Sirloin Restaurants	52058	$4,665.60
47	1/29/20X3	Elkhorn Coffee Shops	24701	$72.67
48	1/29/20X3	Granny's Café	40435	$3,744.00
49	1/29/20X3	High Country Coffee	68752	$40.32
50	1/29/20X3	High Country Coffee	68752	$5,805.60
51	1/29/20X3	Julie's Wraps	59316	$1,610.40
52	1/29/20X3	Mile High Steakhouses	66286	$78.57
53	1/29/20X3	Smokey's Barbeque Pit	86485	$33.07
54	1/30/20X3	Luigi's Bistro	43288	$10.37
55	1/30/20X3	Mountain Lion Restaurant	12295	$3,376.80
56	1/30/20X3	Mountain Trout Fish House	72609	$23.85
57	1/30/2003	Scotty's Taverns	43075	$2,272.80
58	1/30/2003	Smokey's Barbeque Pit	86485	$4,761.60

Client Supporting Document

Alpine Cupcakes, Inc.
Mailroom Control Listing
January 20X3

Item No.	Date	Customer Name	Customer Number	Amount
59	1/30/2003	St. Francis Hotel and Spa	46367	$5,604.00
60	1/30/2003	The Breakfast Place	50226	$4,116.00
61	1/31/2003	Boulder Tea House	58300	$4.02
62	1/31/2003	Elkhorn Coffee Shops	24701	$10,464.00
63	1/31/2003	Fontana Catering & Café	33692	$3,434.40
64	1/31/2003	UC Denver Food Service	40669	$78.95
65				
66				
67				
68				
69				
70				
71				
72				
73				
74				
75				
76				
77				
78				
79				
80				

Monthly Reconciliation:

Total Received—January 20X3	121,358.75
Total per the Cash Receipts Journal	151,358.75
Subtract Storefront Cash Receipts	30,000.00
Total Customer Receipts per General Ledger	121,358.75
Difference:	0.00

Signature of Reconciler: _____Lindsay McKenna_____   Date: _2/06/2X3_

Client Supporting Document

Performed by:
TES 02/01/20X3
Reviewed by:
SDM 2/7/20x3

General Ledger

No.	Date	Dr	Cr.	Acct #	Acct Name
7993	1/2/2003	$9,158.40		1101	Cash: Corporate Accounts
		AR.5.2	$9,158.40	1200	Accounts Receivable

General Ledger

No.	Date	Dr	Cr.	acct #	Acct Name
7998	1/2/2003	$1,591.20		1101	Cash: Corporate Accounts
		AR.5.6	$1,591.20	1200	Accounts Receivable

Garcia and Foster, CPAs

Performed By: *TES*   **Reviewed By:** SDM
Date: *02/13/20X3*   **Date:** 2/15/20x3

Client: Alpine Cupcakes, Inc.
Year End: 12/31/20X2

We performed the sales cutoff testing as of 12/31/20X2. We randomly selected 2 corporate sales customer accounts to perform the cutoff testing. The following customers were selected from the December 20X2 sales journal:

Customer Name	Workpaper Ref. No.	Testing Period	Sales Date	Sales Amount	
Smokey's Barbeque Pit	AR.6.2	Before year end	12/31/20X2	$4,761.60	
Smokey's Barbeque Pit	AR.6.3	After year end	1/31/20X3	$3,532.80	
Country Barrel Restaurant	AR.6.4	Before year end	12/31/20X2	$8,452.80	
Country Barrel Restaurant	AR.6.5	After year end	1/31/20X3	$6,727.20	

Since the company records all transactions at the end of the month, we requested the following documentation: customer purchase order, monthly product invoice, and monthly shipping invoice for each customer in December and January. The total amount of revenue on the customer purchase orders and product invoices ties to the sales amount identified for each customer. We tied the total of items shipped per the shipping invoices and product invoices to the customer purchase order. We requested the shipping reports for the customers and retained copies of the shipping reports that occurred 5 days before or 5 days after year end. We tied the items shipped five days before or five days after year end to the shipping invoices. Through examining these documents, we identified that all of the transactions existed and were recorded in the right period.

Since all cupcakes are delivered on the day the items are shipped, there are no issues with the shipping terms. Alpine Cupcakes records all transactions on the last day of the month. Since all transactions were shipped and received by the customer in that month, the final month's transactions are recorded in the right period.

Garcia and Foster Audit Workpaper   AR.6.1: pg. 1 of 1

Performed by:
TES 02/13/20X3
Reviewed by:
SDM 2/15/20x3

PURCHASE ORDER

Smokey's Barbeque Pit
7700 East Hampden Avenue
Denver, CO 80231

Purchased From:

Alpine Cupcakes
1250 16th Street
Denver, CO 80202

Purchase Order:	1842
Date:	12/2/20X2
Page:	1

	Ordered	Unit	Description	Tax	Unit Price	Total
√	198	cupcake	Carrot Cake		$2.40	$475.20
	377	cupcake	Chocolate		$2.40	$904.80
	119	cupcake	Gluten-free Chocolate		$2.40	$285.60
	258	cupcake	Lemon		$2.40	$619.20
	139	cupcake	Red Velvet		$2.40	$333.60
	139	cupcake	Spice		$2.40	$333.60
	695	cupcake	Vanilla		$2.40	$1,668.00
	59	cupcake	Almond Vegan		$2.40	$141.60

Purchase Approved By: *Kenneth Monson*

Purchase Approval Date: _12/2/20x2_

Total Amount $4,761. 60   AR.6.1

PMT Received
1/30/20X3

Lindsay McKenna
Alpine Shipping Slip Numbers: **27720, 27735, 27752, 27798, 27817, 27836, 27942, 28004**
Alpine Invoice Number: **6461**

Auditor Notes:
√ - *tied amounts to product invoice and to the shipping invoices.*

PRODUCT INVOICE

Alpine Cupcakes, Inc.
1250 16th Street
Denver, Colorado 80202

Page 1/4

Shipped To:

Smokey's Barbeque Pit

7700 E Hampden Ave.

Denver, CO 80231

Customer PO: 1842

Customer PO Date: 12/02/20X2

Invoice Number: 6461

Date: 12/31/20X2

Due Date: 1/30/20X3

Sales Order No: 2784

No. Ordered	Date Shipped	No. Shipped	No. Left in Order	Description	Price	Total
198	12/3/20X2	25 √	173	Carrot Cake	$2.40	$60.00
377	12/3/20X2	47	330	Chocolate	$2.40	$112.80
119	12/3/20X2	15	104	Gluten-free Choc.	$2.40	$36.00
258	12/3/20X2	32	226	Lemon	$2.40	$76.80
139	12/3/20X2	17	122	Red Velvet	$2.40	$40.80
139	12/3/20X2	17	122	Spice	$2.40	$40.80
695	12/3/20X2	87	608	Vanilla	$2.40	$208.80
59	12/3/20X2	7	52	Almond Vegan	$2.40	$16.80
				Shipment Total		**$592.80**
198	12/8/20X2	25	148	Carrot Cake	$2.40	$60.00
377	12/8/20X2	47	283	Chocolate	$2.40	$112.80
119	12/8/20X2	15	89	Gluten-free Choc.	$2.40	$36.00
258	12/8/20X2	32	194	Lemon	$2.40	$76.80
139	12/8/20X2	17	105	Red Velvet	$2.40	$40.80
139	12/8/20X2	17	105	Spice	$2.40	$40.80
695	12/8/20X2	87	521	Vanilla	$2.40	$208.80
59	12/8/20X2	7	45	Almond Vegan	$2.40	$16.80
				Shipment Total		**$592.80**
198	12/12/20X2	25	123	Carrot Cake	$2.40	$60.00
377	12/12/20X2	47	236	Chocolate	$2.40	$112.80
119	12/12/20X2	15	74	Gluten-free Choc.	$2.40	$36.00
258	12/12/20X2	32	162	Lemon	$2.40	$76.80
139	12/12/20X2	17	88	Red Velvet	$2.40	$40.80
139	12/12/20X2	17	88	Spice	$2.40	$40.80
695	12/12/20X2	87	434	Vanilla	$2.40	$208.80
59	12/12/20X2	7	38	Almond Vegan	$2.40	$16.80
				Shipment Total		**$592.80**

Client Supporting Document

AR.6.2: pg. 2 of 11

Performed by:
TES 02/13/20X3
Reviewed by:
SDM 2/15/20x3

PRODUCT INVOICE (continued)

Alpine Cupcakes, Inc.
1250 16th Street
Denver, Colorado 80202

Page 2/4

Shipped To:

Smokey's Barbeque Pit

7700 E Hampden Ave.

Denver, CO 80231

Invoice Number: 6461

Date: 12/31/20X2

Ordered	Date Shipped	No. Shipped		No. Left in Order	Description	Price	Total
198	12/16/20X2	25	√	98	Carrot Cake	$2.40	$60.00
377	12/16/20X2	47		189	Chocolate	$2.40	$112.80
119	12/16/20X2	15		59	Gluten-free Choc.	$2.40	$36.00
258	12/16/20X2	32		130	Lemon	$2.40	$76.80
139	12/16/20X2	17		71	Red Velvet	$2.40	$40.80
139	12/16/20X2	17		71	Spice	$2.40	$40.80
695	12/16/20X2	87		347	Vanilla	$2.40	$208.80
59	12/16/20X2	7		31	Almond Vegan	$2.40	$16.80
					Shipment Total		**$592.80**
198	12/21/20X2	25		73	Carrot Cake	$2.40	$60.00
377	12/21/20X2	47		142	Chocolate	$2.40	$112.80
119	12/21/20X2	15		44	Gluten-free Choc.	$2.40	$36.00
258	12/21/20X2	32		98	Lemon	$2.40	$76.80
139	12/21/20X2	17		54	Red Velvet	$2.40	$40.80
139	12/21/20X2	17		54	Spice	$2.40	$40.80
695	12/21/20X2	87		260	Vanilla	$2.40	$208.80
59	12/21/20X2	7		24	Almond Vegan	$2.40	$16.80
					Shipment Total		**$592.80**
198	12/26/20X2	25		48	Carrot Cake	$2.40	$60.00
377	12/26/20X2	47		95	Chocolate	$2.40	$112.80
119	12/26/20X2	15		29	Gluten-free Choc.	$2.40	$36.00
258	12/26/20X2	32		66	Lemon	$2.40	$76.80
139	12/26/20X2	17		37	Red Velvet	$2.40	$40.80
139	12/26/20X2	17		37	Spice	$2.40	$40.80
695	12/26/20X2	87		173	Vanilla	$2.40	$208.80
59	12/26/20X2	7	↓	17	Almond Vegan	$2.40	$16.80
					Shipment Total		**$592.80**

Performed by:
TES 02/13/20X3
Reviewed by:
SDM 2/15/20x3

PRODUCT INVOICE (continued)

Alpine Cupcakes, Inc.
1250 16th Street
Denver, Colorado 80202

Page 3/4

Shipped To:

Smokey's Barbeque Pit

7700 E Hampden Ave.

Denver, CO 80231

Invoice Number: 6461

Date: 12/31/20X2

Ordered	Date Shipped	No. Shipped	No. Left in Order	Description	Price	Total
198	12/29/20X2	25	23	Carrot Cake	$2.40	$60.00
377	12/29/20X2	47	48	Chocolate	$2.40	$112.80
119	12/29/20X2	15	14	Gluten-free Choc.	$2.40	$36.00
258	12/29/20X2	32	34	Lemon	$2.40	$76.80
139	12/29/20X2	17	20	Red Velvet	$2.40	$40.80
139	12/29/20X2	17	20	Spice	$2.40	$40.80
695	12/29/20X2	87	86	Vanilla	$2.40	$208.80
59	12/29/20X2	7	10	Almond Vegan	$2.40	$16.80
				Shipment Total		**$592.80**
198	1/02/20X3	23	0	Carrot Cake	$2.40	$55.20
377	1/02/20X3	48	0	Chocolate	$2.40	$115.20
119	1/02/20X3	14	0	Gluten-free Choc.	$2.40	$33.60
258	1/02/20X3	34	0	Lemon	$2.40	$81.60
139	1/02/20X3	20	0	Red Velvet	$2.40	$48.00
139	1/02/20X3	20	0	Spice	$2.40	$48.00
695	1/02/20X3	86	0	Vanilla	$2.40	$206.40
59	1/02/20X3	10	0	Almond Vegan	$2.40	$24.00
				Shipment Total		**$612.00**

Sales Tax	N/A
Freight	N/A
Invoice Total	$4,761.60

AR.6.1

Performed by:
TES 02/13/20X3
Reviewed by:
SDM 2/15/20x3

Please return this page with your payment

PRODUCT INVOICE

Remittance Advice

Smokey's Barbeque Pit
7700 E Hampden Ave.
Denver, CO 80231

Page 4/4

Invoice Number:	6461
Sales Order No:	2784
Customer PO:	1842
Customer PO Date:	12/02/20X2
Total Amount Owed:	$4,761.60
Date Due:	1/30/20X3

Date Paid   _____

Amount Paid   _____

Pmt Received

1/30/20X3

Lindsay McKenna

See returned remittance form

Auditor Notes:
Calculated totals and tied amounts to customer purchase order and shipping invoice.

Carrot Cake = 198	√	Red Velvet = 139	√
Chocolate = 377	√	Spice = 139	√
Gluten-free Chocolate = 119	√	Vanilla = 695	√
Lemon = 258	√	Almond Vegan = 59	√

Alpine Cupcakes, Inc.
Sales Cutoff Testing
Smokey's Before Year End

SHIPPING INVOICE

Alpine Cupcakes, Inc.
1250 16th Street
Denver, Colorado 80202

Page 1/4

Shipped To:

Smokey's Barbeque Pit

7700 E Hampden Ave., Denver, CO 80231

Customer PO: 1842   Customer PO Date: 12/02/20X2

Ship Invoice Number: S6461

Date: 12/31/20X2

Due Date: 1/30/20X3

Sales Order No: 2784

Shipping Report # 27720

No. Ordered	Date Shipped		Dozen Shipped	Description	Price per Dozen	Total
198	12/3/20X2	√	2.08	Carrot Cake	$0.20	$0.42
377	12/3/20X2		3.92	Chocolate	$0.20	$0.78
119	12/3/20X2		1.25	Gluten-free Choc.	$0.20	$0.25
258	12/3/20X2		2.67	Lemon	$0.20	$0.53
139	12/3/20X2		1.42	Red Velvet	$0.20	$0.28
139	12/3/20X2		1.42	Spice	$0.20	$0.28
695	12/3/20X2		7.25	Vanilla	$0.20	$1.45
59	12/3/20X2		0.58	Almond Vegan	$0.20	$0.12
Total Shipped			**21**	**Price per Dozen**	**$0.20**	**$4.12**

Shipping Report # 27735

No. Ordered	Date Shipped	Dozen Shipped	Description	Price per Dozen	Total
198	12/8/20X2	2.08	Carrot Cake	$0.20	$0.42
377	12/8/20X2	3.92	Chocolate	$0.20	$0.78
119	12/8/20X2	1.25	Gluten-free Choc.	$0.20	$0.25
258	12/8/20X2	2.67	Lemon	$0.20	$0.53
139	12/8/20X2	1.42	Red Velvet	$0.20	$0.28
139	12/8/20X2	1.42	Spice	$0.20	$0.28
695	12/8/20X2	7.25	Vanilla	$0.20	$1.45
59	12/8/20X2	0.58	Almond Vegan	$0.20	$0.12
Total Shipped		**21**	**Price per Dozen**	**$0.20**	**$4.12**

Shipping Report # 27752

No. Ordered	Date Shipped	Dozen Shipped	Description	Price per Dozen	Total
198	12/12/20X2	2.08	Carrot Cake	$0.20	$0.42
377	12/12/20X2	3.92	Chocolate	$0.20	$0.78
119	12/12/20X2	1.25	Gluten-free Choc.	$0.20	$0.25
258	12/12/20X2	2.67	Lemon	$0.20	$0.53
139	12/12/20X2	1.42	Red Velvet	$0.20	$0.28
139	12/12/20X2	1.42	Spice	$0.20	$0.28
695	12/12/20X2	7.25	Vanilla	$0.20	$1.45
59	12/12/20X2	0.58	Almond Vegan	$0.20	$0.12
Total Shipped		**21**	**Price per Dozen**	**$0.20**	**$4.12**

Performed by:
TES 02/13/20X3
Reviewed by:
SDM 2/15/20X3

SHIPPING INVOICE (continued)

Alpine Cupcakes, Inc.
1250 16th Street
Denver, Colorado 80202

Page 2/4

Shipped To:

Ship Invoice Number: S6461

Smokey's Barbeque Pit

Date: 12/31/20X2

7700 E Hampden Ave., Denver, CO 80231

Shipping Report # 27798

Ordered	Date Shipped	Dozen Shipped	Description	Price per Dozen	Total
198	12/16/20X2 √	2.08	Carrot Cake	$0.20	$0.42
377	12/16/20X2	3.92	Chocolate	$0.20	$0.78
119	12/16/20X2	1.25	Gluten-free Choc.	$0.20	$0.25
258	12/16/20X2	2.67	Lemon	$0.20	$0.53
139	12/16/20X2	1.42	Red Velvet	$0.20	$0.28
139	12/16/20X2	1.42	Spice	$0.20	$0.28
695	12/16/20X2	7.25	Vanilla	$0.20	$1.45
59	12/16/20X2	0.58	Almond Vegan	$0.20	$0.12
	Total Shipped	**20.59**	**Price per Dozen**	**$0.20**	**$4.12**

Shipping Report # 27817

Ordered	Date Shipped	Dozen Shipped	Description	Price per Dozen	Total
198	12/21/20X2	2.08	Carrot Cake	$0.20	$0.42
377	12/21/20X2	3.92	Chocolate	$0.20	$0.78
119	12/21/20X2	1.25	Gluten-free Choc.	$0.20	$0.25
258	12/21/20X2	2.67	Lemon	$0.20	$0.53
139	12/21/20X2	1.42	Red Velvet	$0.20	$0.28
139	12/21/20X2	1.42	Spice	$0.20	$0.28
695	12/21/20X2	7.25	Vanilla	$0.20	$1.45
59	12/21/20X2	0.58	Almond Vegan	$0.20	$0.12
	Total Shipped	**20.59**	**Price per Dozen**	**$0.20**	**$4.12**

Shipping Report # 27836

Ordered	Date Shipped	Dozen Shipped	Description	Price per Dozen	Total
198	12/26/20X2	2.08 μ	Carrot Cake	$0.20	$0.42
377	12/26/20X2	3.92	Chocolate	$0.20	$0.78
119	12/26/20X2	1.25	Gluten-free Choc.	$0.20	$0.25
258	12/26/20X2	2.67	Lemon	$0.20	$0.53
139	12/26/20X2	1.42	Red Velvet	$0.20	$0.28
139	12/26/20X2	1.42	Spice	$0.20	$0.28
695	12/26/20X2	7.25	Vanilla	$0.20	$1.45
59	12/26/20X2	0.58	Almond Vegan	$0.20	$0.12
	Total Shipped	**20.59**	**Price per Dozen**	**$0.20**	**$4.12**

Client Supporting Document

AR.6.2: pg. 7 of 11

SHIPPING INVOICE (continued)

Alpine Cupcakes, Inc.
1250 16th Street
Denver, Colorado 80202

Page 3/4

Shipped To:

Smokey's Barbeque Pit
7700 E Hampden Ave.
Denver, CO 80231

Ship Invoice Number: S6461

Date: 12/31/20X2

Shipping Report # 27942

Ordered	Date Shipped	Dozen Shipped	Description	Price per Dozen	Total
198	12/29/20X2	2.08	Carrot Cake	$0.20	$0.42
377	12/29/20X2	3.92	Chocolate	$0.20	$0.78
119	12/29/20X2	1.25	Gluten-free Choc.	$0.20	$0.25
258	12/29/20X2	2.67	Lemon	$0.20	$0.53
139	12/29/20X2	1.42	Red Velvet	$0.20	$0.28
139	12/29/20X2	1.42	Spice	$0.20	$0.28
695	12/29/20X2	7.25	Vanilla	$0.20	$1.45
59	12/29/20X2	0.58	Almond Vegan	$0.20	$0.12
	Total Shipped	**20.59**	**Price per Dozen**	**$0.20**	**$4.12**

Shipping Report # 28004

Ordered	Date Shipped	Dozen Shipped	Description	Price per Dozen	Total
198	1/02/20X3	1.92	Carrot Cake	$0.20	$0.38
377	1/02/20X3	4.00	Chocolate	$0.20	$0.80
119	1/02/20X3	1.17	Gluten-free Choc.	$0.20	$0.23
258	1/02/20X3	2.83	Lemon	$0.20	$0.57
139	1/02/20X3	1.67	Red Velvet	$0.20	$0.33
139	1/02/20X3	1.67	Spice	$0.20	$0.33
695	1/02/20X3	7.17	Vanilla	$0.20	$1.43
59	1/02/20X3	0.83	Almond Vegan	$0.20	$0.17
	Total Shipped	**21.26**	**Price per Dozen**	**$0.20**	**$4.25**

Sales Tax		N/A
Invoice Total		$33.07

Performed by:
TES 02/13/20X3
Reviewed by:
SDM 2/15/20x3

Please return this page with your payment

SHIPPING INVOICE

Remittance Advice

Smokey's Barbeque Pit
7700 E Hampden Ave.
Denver, CO 80231

Page 4/4

Invoice Number:	S6461
Sales Order No:	2784
Customer PO:	1842
Customer PO Date:	12/02/20X2
Amount Due:	$33.07
Date Due:	1/30/20X3

Date Paid _____

Amount Paid _____

Pmt
Received
1/29/20X3

Lindsay McKenna

See returned remittance form

Auditor Notes:

Sum of Items Shipped: Calculated totals by adding up the Dozen Shipped per cupcake type and then multiplying by 12. Tied totals per cupcake type to customer purchase order and product invoice.

*Carrot Cake = 16.48 * 12 = 198* √   *Red Velvet = 11.61 * 12 = 139* √

*Chocolate = 31.44 * 12 = 377* √   *Spice = 11.61 * 12 = 139* √

*Gluten-free Chocolate = 9.92 * 12 = 119* √   *Vanilla = 57.92 * 12 = 695* √

*Lemon = 21.52 * 12 = 258* √   *Almond Vegan = 4.89 * 12 = 59* √

Calculated totals of items shipped 5 days before year end by adding up the dozens of items shipped by cupcake type multiplied by 12. Amounts were tied to the shipping reports.

*Carrot Cake = 6.08 * 12 = 73* μ   *Red Velvet = 4.51 * 12 = 54* μ

*Chocolate = 11.84 * 12 = 142* μ   *Spice = 4.51 * 12 = 54* μ

*Gluten-free Chocolate = 3.67 * 12 = 44* μ   *Vanilla = 21.67 * 12 = 260* μ

*Lemon = 8.17 * 12 = 98* μ   *Almond Vegan = 1.99 * 12 = 24* μ

Client Supporting Document

| Performed by: |
| TES 02/13/20X3 |
| Reviewed by: |
| SDM 2/15/20x3 |

ALPINE CUPCAKES, INC.

Shipping Report

Date: 12/26/20X2

Purchase Order #: 1842

Shipping Report # 27836

Shipped To: Smokey's Barbeque Pit

Freight Carrier: Alpine Cupcake Carrier

Quantity	Unit	Description
25 μ	Cupcakes	Carrot Cake
47	Cupcakes	Chocolate
15	Cupcakes	Gluten-free Chocolate
32	Cupcakes	Lemon
17	Cupcakes	Red Velvet
17	Cupcakes	Spice
87	Cupcakes	Vanilla
7	Cupcakes	Almond Vegan

Remarks: Items received in OK condition

Received By: Rocco Fazio

Delivered To: Receiving Dept.

ALPINE CUPCAKES, INC.

Shipping Report

Date: 12/29/20X2

Purchase Order #: 1842

Shipping Report # 27942

Shipped To: Smokey's Barbeque Pit

Freight Carrier: Alpine Cupcake Carrier

Quantity	Unit	Description
25 μ	Cupcakes	Carrot Cake
47	Cupcakes	Chocolate
15	Cupcakes	Gluten-free Chocolate
32	Cupcakes	Lemon
17	Cupcakes	Red Velvet
17	Cupcakes	Spice
87	Cupcakes	Vanilla
7	Cupcakes	Almond Vegan

Remarks: Items received in OK condition

Received By: Rocco Fazio

Delivered To: Receiving Dept.

Alpine Cupcakes, Inc.
Sales Cutoff Testing
Smokey's Before Year End

Performed by:
TES 02/13/20X3
Reviewed by:
SDM 2/15/20x3

ALPINE CUPCAKES, INC.

Shipping Report

Date: 1/02/20X3

Purchase Order #: 1842

Shipping Report # 28004

Shipped To: Smokey's Barbeque Pit

Freight Carrier: Alpine Cupcake Carrier

Quantity	Unit	Description
23 μ	Cupcakes	Carrot Cake
48	Cupcakes	Chocolate
14	Cupcakes	Gluten-free Chocolate
34	Cupcakes	Lemon
20	Cupcakes	Red Velvet
20	Cupcakes	Spice
86	Cupcakes	Vanilla
10	Cupcakes	Almond Vegan

Remarks: Items received in OK condition

Received By: Rocco Fazio

Delivered To: Receiving Dept.

Auditor Notes:

Calculated totals of items shipped 5 days before year end by adding up the number of items shipped by cupcake type. Amounts were tied to the shipping invoice.

Carrot Cake = 73 μ   Red Velvet = 54 μ

Chocolate = 142 μ   Spice = 54 μ

Gluten-free Chocolate = 44 μ   Vanilla = 260 μ

Lemon = 98 μ   Almond Vegan = 24 μ

Client Supporting Document

AR.6.2: pg. 11 of 11

190

Performed by:
TES 02/13/20X3
Reviewed by:
SDM 2/15/20x3

PURCHASE ORDER

Smokey's Barbeque Pit
7700 East Hampden Avenue
Denver, CO 80231

Purchased From:
Alpine Cupcakes
1250 16th Street
Denver, CO 80202

Purchase Order: 1857
Date: 1/3/20X3
Page: 1

	Ordered	Unit	Description	Tax	Unit Price	Total
√	206	cupcake	Carrot Cake		$2.40	$494.40
	339	cupcake	Chocolate		$2.40	$813.60
	147	cupcake	Gluten-free Chocolate		$2.40	$352.80
	177	cupcake	Lemon		$2.40	$424.80
	132	cupcake	Red Velvet		$2.40	$316.80
	162	cupcake	Spice		$2.40	$388.80
	29	cupcake	Almond Vegan		$2.40	$69.60

Purchase Approved By: *Kenneth Monson*

Purchase Approval Date: *1/3/20x3*

Total Amount $2,860.80

PMT Received 2/10/20X3

Lindsay McKenna
Alpine Shipping slip Numbers: **28040, 28098, 28124, 28168, 28192, 28217, 28262, 28313**
Alpine Invoice Number: **6494**

Auditor Notes:
√ - *tied amounts to product invoice and to the shipping invoices.*

Performed by:
TES 02/13/20X3
Reviewed by:
SDM 2/15/20x3

PRODUCT INVOICE

Alpine Cupcakes, Inc.
1250 16th Street
Denver, Colorado 80202

Page 1/4

Shipped To:

Smokey's Barbeque Pit

7700 E Hampden Ave.

Denver, CO 80231

Customer PO: 1857

Customer PO Date: 1/3/20X3

Invoice Number: 6494

Date: 1/31/20X3

Due Date: 3/1/20X3

Sales Order No: 2817

No. Ordered	Date Shipped	No. Shipped	No. Left in Order	Description	Price	Total
206	1/3/20X3	26 √	180	Carrot Cake	$2.40	$62.40
339	1/3/20X3	42	297	Chocolate	$2.40	$100.80
147	1/3/20X3	18	129	Gluten-free Choc.	$2.40	$43.20
177	1/3/20X3	22	155	Lemon	$2.40	$52.80
132	1/3/20X3	17	115	Red Velvet	$2.40	$40.80
162	1/3/20X3	20	142	Spice	$2.40	$48.00
280	1/3/20X3	35	245	Vanilla	$2.40	$84.00
29	1/3/20X3	4	25	Almond Vegan	$2.40	$9.60
				Shipment Total		**$441.60**
206	1/9/20X3	26	154	Carrot Cake	$2.40	$62.40
339	1/9/20X3	42	255	Chocolate	$2.40	$100.80
147	1/9/20X3	18	111	Gluten-free Choc.	$2.40	$43.20
177	1/9/20X3	22	133	Lemon	$2.40	$52.80
132	1/9/20X3	17	98	Red Velvet	$2.40	$40.80
162	1/9/20X3	20	122	Spice	$2.40	$48.00
280	1/9/20X3	35	210	Vanilla	$2.40	$84.00
29	1/9/20X3	4	21	Almond Vegan	$2.40	$9.60
				Shipment Total		**$441.60**
206	1/14/20X3	26	128	Carrot Cake	$2.40	$62.40
339	1/14/20X3	42	213	Chocolate	$2.40	$100.80
147	1/14/20X3	18	93	Gluten-free Choc.	$2.40	$43.20
177	1/14/20X3	22	111	Lemon	$2.40	$52.80
132	1/14/20X3	17	81	Red Velvet	$2.40	$40.80
162	1/14/20X3	20	102	Spice	$2.40	$48.00
280	1/14/20X3	35	175	Vanilla	$2.40	$84.00
29	1/14/20X3	4	17	Almond Vegan	$2.40	$9.60
				Shipment Total		**$441.60**

Performed by:
TES 02/13/20X3
Reviewed by:
SDM 2/15/20x3

PRODUCT INVOICE (continued)

Alpine Cupcakes, Inc.
1250 16th Street
Denver, Colorado 80202

Page 2/4

Shipped To:

Smokey's Barbeque Pit

7700 E Hampden Ave.

Denver, CO 80231

Invoice Number: 6494

Date: 1/31/20X3

Ordered	Date Shipped	No. Shipped		No. Left in Order	Description	Price	Total
206	1/20/20X3	26	√	102	Carrot Cake	$2.40	$62.40
339	1/20/20X3	42		171	Chocolate	$2.40	$100.80
147	1/20/20X3	18		75	Gluten-free Choc.	$2.40	$43.20
177	1/20/20X3	22		89	Lemon	$2.40	$52.80
132	1/20/20X3	17		64	Red Velvet	$2.40	$40.80
162	1/20/20X3	20		82	Spice	$2.40	$48.00
280	1/20/20X3	35		140	Vanilla	$2.40	$84.00
29	1/20/20X3	4		13	Almond Vegan	$2.40	$9.60
					Shipment Total		**$441.60**
206	1/24/20X3	26		76	Carrot Cake	$2.40	$62.40
339	1/24/20X3	42		129	Chocolate	$2.40	$100.80
147	1/24/20X3	18		57	Gluten-free Choc.	$2.40	$43.20
177	1/24/20X3	22		67	Lemon	$2.40	$52.80
132	1/24/20X3	17		47	Red Velvet	$2.40	$40.80
162	1/24/20X3	20		62	Spice	$2.40	$48.00
280	1/24/20X3	35		105	Vanilla	$2.40	$84.00
29	1/24/20X3	4		9	Almond Vegan	$2.40	$9.60
					Shipment Total		**$441.60**
206	1/26/20X3	26		50	Carrot Cake	$2.40	$62.40
339	1/26/20X3	42		87	Chocolate	$2.40	$100.80
147	1/26/20X3	18		39	Gluten-free Choc.	$2.40	$43.20
177	1/26/20X3	22		45	Lemon	$2.40	$52.80
132	1/26/20X3	17		30	Red Velvet	$2.40	$40.80
162	1/26/20X3	20		42	Spice	$2.40	$48.00
280	1/26/20X3	35		70	Vanilla	$2.40	$84.00
29	1/26/20X3	4		5	Almond Vegan	$2.40	$9.60
					Shipment Total		**$441.60**

<table>
<tr><td>Performed by:
TES 02/13/20X3
Reviewed by:
SDM 2/15/20x3</td></tr>
</table>

PRODUCT INVOICE (continued)

Alpine Cupcakes, Inc.
1250 16th Street
Denver, Colorado 80202

Page 3/4
Invoice Number: 6494
Date: 1/31/20X3

Shipped To:

Smokey's Barbeque Pit
7700 E Hampden Ave.
Denver, CO 80231

Ordered	Date Shipped	No. Shipped	No. Left in Order	Description	Price	Total
206	1/28/20X3	26 √	24	Carrot Cake	$2.40	$62.40
339	1/28/20X3	42	45	Chocolate	$2.40	$100.80
147	1/28/20X3	18	21	Gluten-free Choc.	$2.40	$43.20
177	1/28/20X3	22	23	Lemon	$2.40	$52.80
132	1/28/20X3	17	13	Red Velvet	$2.40	$40.80
162	1/28/20X3	20	22	Spice	$2.40	$48.00
280	1/28/20X3	35	35	Vanilla	$2.40	$84.00
29	1/28/20X3	4	1	Almond Vegan	$2.40	$9.60
				Shipment Total		**$441.60**
206	2/01/20X3	24	0	Carrot Cake	$2.40	$57.60
339	2/01/20X3	45	0	Chocolate	$2.40	$108.00
147	2/01/20X3	21	0	Gluten-free Choc.	$2.40	$50.40
177	2/01/20X3	23	0	Lemon	$2.40	$55.20
132	2/01/20X3	13	0	Red Velvet	$2.40	$31.20
162	2/01/20X3	22	0	Spice	$2.40	$52.80
280	2/01/20X3	35	0	Vanilla	$2.40	$84.00
29	2/01/20X3	1	0	Almond Vegan	$2.40	$2.40
				Shipment Total		**$441.60**

Sales Tax	N/A
Freight	N/A
Invoice Total	$3,532.80

AR.6.1

Performed by:
TES 02/13/20X3
Reviewed by:
SDM 2/15/20x3

Please return this page with your payment

PRODUCT INVOICE

Remittance Advice

Smokey's Barbeque Pit
7700 E Hampden Ave.
Denver, CO 80231

Page 4/4

Invoice Number:	6494
Sales Order No:	2817
Customer PO:	1857
Customer PO Date:	1/03/20X3
Total Amount Owed:	$3,532.80
Date Due:	3/01/20X3

Date Paid _____

Amount Paid _____

Pmt Received
2/10/20X3

Lindsay McKenna

See returned remittance form

Auditor Notes:
Calculated totals and tied amounts to customer purchase order and shipping invoice.

Carrot Cake = 206 √	*Red Velvet = 132* √
Chocolate = 339 √	*Spice = 162* √
Gluten-free Chocolate = 147 √	*Vanilla = 280* √
Lemon = 177 √	*Almond Vegan = 29* √

Alpine Cupcakes, Inc.
Sales Cutoff Testing
Smokey's After Year End

Performed by:
TES 02/13/20X3
Reviewed by:
SDM 2/15/20x3

SHIPPING INVOICE

Alpine Cupcakes, Inc.
1250 16th Street
Denver, Colorado 80202

Page 1/4

Shipped To:

Smokey's Barbeque Pit

7700 E Hampden Ave., Denver, CO 80231

Customer PO: 1857   Customer PO Date: 1/03/20X3

Ship Invoice Number: S6494

Date: 1/31/20X3

Due Date: 3/02/20X3

Sales Order No: 2817

Shipping Report # 28040

No. Ordered	Date Shipped	Dozen Shipped	Description	Price per Dozen	Total
206	1/3/20X3	√ 2.17 μ	Carrot Cake	$0.20	$0.43
339	1/3/20X3	3.50	Chocolate	$0.20	$0.70
147	1/3/20X3	1.50	Gluten-free Choc.	$0.20	$0.30
177	1/3/20X3	1.83	Lemon	$0.20	$0.37
132	1/3/20X3	1.42	Red Velvet	$0.20	$0.28
162	1/3/20X3	1.67	Spice	$0.20	$0.33
280	1/3/20X3	2.92	Vanilla	$0.20	$0.58
29	1/3/20X3	0.33	Almond Vegan	$0.20	$0.07
	Total Shipped	15.34	**Price per Dozen**	**$0.20**	**$3.07**

Shipping Report # 28098

No. Ordered	Date Shipped	Dozen Shipped	Description	Price per Dozen	Total
206	1/9/20X3	2.17	Carrot Cake	$0.20	$0.43
339	1/9/20X3	3.50	Chocolate	$0.20	$0.70
147	1/9/20X3	1.50	Gluten-free Choc.	$0.20	$0.30
177	1/9/20X3	1.83	Lemon	$0.20	$0.37
132	1/9/20X3	1.42	Red Velvet	$0.20	$0.28
162	1/9/20X3	1.67	Spice	$0.20	$0.33
280	1/9/20X3	2.92	Vanilla	$0.20	$0.58
29	1/9/20X3	0.33	Almond Vegan	$0.20	$0.07
	Total Shipped	15.34	**Price per Dozen**	**$0.20**	**$3.07**

Shipping Report # 28124

No. Ordered	Date Shipped	Dozen Shipped	Description	Price per Dozen	Total
206	1/14/20X3	2.17	Carrot Cake	$0.20	$0.43
339	1/14/20X3	3.50	Chocolate	$0.20	$0.70
147	1/14/20X3	1.50	Gluten-free Choc.	$0.20	$0.30
177	1/14/20X3	1.83	Lemon	$0.20	$0.37
132	1/14/20X3	1.42	Red Velvet	$0.20	$0.28
162	1/14/20X3	1.67	Spice	$0.20	$0.33
280	1/14/20X3	2.92	Vanilla	$0.20	$0.58
29	1/14/20X3	0.33	Almond Vegan	$0.20	$0.07
	Total Shipped	15.34	**Price per Dozen**	**$0.20**	**$3.07**

Alpine Cupcakes, Inc.
Sales Cutoff Testing
Smokey's After Year End

SHIPPING INVOICE (continued)

Alpine Cupcakes, Inc.
1250 16th Street
Denver, Colorado 80202

Page 2/4

Shipped To:

Smokey's Barbeque Pit

7700 E Hampden Ave., Denver, CO 80231

Ship Invoice Number: S6494

Date: 1/31/20X3

Shipping Report # 28168

Ordered	Date Shipped	Dozen Shipped	Description	Price per Dozen	Total
206	1/20/20X3 √	2.17	Carrot Cake	$0.20	$0.43
339	1/20/20X3	3.50	Chocolate	$0.20	$0.70
147	1/20/20X3	1.50	Gluten-free Choc.	$0.20	$0.30
177	1/20/20X3	1.83	Lemon	$0.20	$0.37
132	1/20/20X3	1.42	Red Velvet	$0.20	$0.28
162	1/20/20X3	1.67	Spice	$0.20	$0.33
280	1/20/20X3	2.92	Vanilla	$0.20	$0.58
29	1/20/20X3	0.33	Almond Vegan	$0.20	$0.07
	Total Shipped	**15.34**	**Price per Dozen**	**$0.20**	**$3.07**

Shipping Report # 28192

Ordered	Date Shipped	Dozen Shipped	Description	Price per Dozen	Total
206	1/24/20X3	2.17	Carrot Cake	$0.20	$0.43
339	1/24/20X3	3.50	Chocolate	$0.20	$0.70
147	1/24/20X3	1.50	Gluten-free Choc.	$0.20	$0.30
177	1/24/20X3	1.83	Lemon	$0.20	$0.37
132	1/24/20X3	1.42	Red Velvet	$0.20	$0.28
162	1/24/20X3	1.67	Spice	$0.20	$0.33
280	1/24/20X3	2.92	Vanilla	$0.20	$0.58
29	1/24/20X3	0.33	Almond Vegan	$0.20	$0.07
	Total Shipped	**15.34**	**Price per Dozen**	**$0.20**	**$3.07**

Shipping Report # 28217

Ordered	Date Shipped	Dozen Shipped	Description	Price per Dozen	Total
206	1/26/20X3	2.17	Carrot Cake	$0.20	$0.43
339	1/26/20X3	3.50	Chocolate	$0.20	$0.70
147	1/26/20X3	1.50	Gluten-free Choc.	$0.20	$0.30
177	1/26/20X3	1.83	Lemon	$0.20	$0.37
132	1/26/20X3	1.42	Red Velvet	$0.20	$0.28
162	1/26/20X3	1.67	Spice	$0.20	$0.33
280	1/26/20X3	2.92	Vanilla	$0.20	$0.58
29	1/26/20X3	0.33	Almond Vegan	$0.20	$0.07
	Total Shipped √	**15.34**	**Price per Dozen**	**$0.20**	**$3.07**

Performed by:
TES 02/13/20X3
Reviewed by:
SDM 2/15/20x3

SHIPPING INVOICE (continued)

Alpine Cupcakes, Inc.
1250 16th Street
Denver, Colorado 80202

Page 3/4

Ship Invoice Number: S6494

Date: 1/31/20X3

Shipped To:

Smokey's Barbeque Pit

7700 E Hampden Ave., Denver, CO 80231

Shipping Report # 28262

Ordered	Date Shipped		Dozen Shipped	Description	Price per Dozen	Total
206	1/28/20X3	√	2.17	Carrot Cake	$0.20	$0.43
339	1/28/20X3		3.50	Chocolate	$0.20	$0.70
147	1/28/20X3		1.50	Gluten-free Choc.	$0.20	$0.30
177	1/28/20X3		1.83	Lemon	$0.20	$0.37
132	1/28/20X3		1.42	Red Velvet	$0.20	$0.28
162	1/28/20X3		1.67	Spice	$0.20	$0.33
280	1/28/20X3		2.92	Vanilla	$0.20	$0.58
29	1/28/20X3		0.33	Almond Vegan	$0.20	$0.07
	Total Shipped		**15.34**	**Price per Dozen**	**$0.20**	**$3.07**

Shipping Report # 28313

Ordered	Date Shipped		Dozen Shipped	Description	Price per Dozen	Total
206	1/29/20X3		2.00	Carrot Cake	$0.20	$0.40
339	1/29/20X3		3.75	Chocolate	$0.20	$0.75
147	1/29/20X3		1.75	Gluten-free Choc.	$0.20	$0.35
177	1/29/20X3		1.92	Lemon	$0.20	$0.38
132	1/29/20X3		1.08	Red Velvet	$0.20	$0.22
162	1/29/20X3		1.83	Spice	$0.20	$0.37
280	1/29/20X3		2.92	Vanilla	$0.20	$0.58
29	1/29/20X3		0.08	Almond Vegan	$0.20	$0.02
	Total Shipped		**15.33**	**Price per Dozen**	**$0.20**	**$3.07**

Sales Tax   N/A

Invoice Total $24.53

Alpine Cupcakes, Inc.
Sales Cutoff Testing
Smokey's After Year End

| Performed by: |
| TES 02/13/20X3 |
| Reviewed by: |
| SDM 2/15/20x3 |

Auditor Notes:

Sum of Items Shipped: Calculated totals by adding up the Dozen Shipped per cupcake type and then multiplying by 12. Tied totals per cupcake type to customer purchase order and product invoice.

Carrot Cake = 17.19 * 12 = 206   √   Red Velvet = 11.02 * 12 = 132   √

Chocolate = 28.25 * 12 = 339   √   Spice = 13.52 * 12 = 162 √

Gluten-free Chocolate = 12.25 * 12 = 147 √   Vanilla = 23.36 * 12 = 280 √

Lemon = 14.73 * 12 = 177 √   Almond Vegan = 2.39 * 12 = 29 √

Calculated totals of items shipped 5 days after year end by adding up the dozens of items shipped by cupcake type multiplied by 12. Amounts were tied to the shipping reports.

Carrot Cake = 2.17 * 12 = 26   μ   Red Velvet = 1.42 * 12 = 17 μ

Chocolate = 3.50 * 12 = 42 μ   Spice = 1.67 * 12 = 20 μ

Gluten-free Chocolate = 1.50 * 12 = 18 μ   Vanilla = 2.92 * 12 = 35 μ

Lemon =   1.83 * 12 = 22 μ   Almond Vegan = 0.33 * 12 = 4 μ

Alpine Cupcakes, Inc.
Sales Cutoff Testing
Smokey's After Year End

Performed by:
TES 02/13/20X3
Reviewed by:
SDM 2/15/20x3

ALPINE CUPCAKES, INC.
Shipping Report

Date: 1/03/20x3
Purchase Order #: 1857
Shipped To: Smokey's Barbeque Pit
Freight Carrier: Alpine Cupcake Carrier

Shipping Report # 28040

Quantity	Unit	Description
26 μ	Cupcakes	Carrot Cake
42	Cupcakes	Chocolate
18	Cupcakes	Gluten-free Chocolate
22	Cupcakes	Lemon
17	Cupcakes	Red Velvet
20	Cupcakes	Spice
35	Cupcakes	Vanilla
4	Cupcakes	Almond Vegan

Remarks: Items received in OK condition
Received By: Rocco Fazio
Delivered To: Receiving Dept.

Auditor Notes:
Calculated totals of items shipped 5 days after year end by adding up the number of items shipped by cupcake type. Amounts were tied to the shipping invoice.

Carrot Cake = 26 μ   Red Velvet = 17 μ
Chocolate = 42 μ   Spice = 20 μ
Gluten-free Chocolate = 18 μ   Almond Vegan = 4 μ
Lemon = 22 μ

Performed by:
TES 02/13/20X3
Reviewed by:
SDM 2/15/20x3

PURCHASE ORDER

Country Barrel Restaurants
1400 Poplar Street
Denver, CO 80224

Purchased From:	
Alpine Cupcakes	
1250 16th Street	
Denver, CO 80202	

Purchase Order:	908
Date:	12/1/20X2
Page:	1

Ordered	Unit	Description	Tax	Unit Price	Total
352	cupcake	Carrot Cake		$2.40	$844.80
670	cupcake	Chocolate		$2.40	$1,608.00
211	cupcake	Gluten-free Chocolate		$2.40	$506.40
458	cupcake	Lemon		$2.40	$1,099.20
246	cupcake	Red Velvet		$2.40	$590.40
246	cupcake	Spice		$2.40	$590.40
1234	cupcake	Vanilla		$2.40	$2,961.60
105	cupcake	Almond Vegan		$2.40	$252.00

Purchase Approved By: *JoAnne Iwertz*

Purchase Approval Date: *12/1/20X2*

Total Amount $8,452.80

AR.6.1

PMT Received
1/27/20X23

Lindsay McKenna
Alpine Shipping slip Numbers: **27731, 27762, 27801, 27827, 27840, 27852, 27954, 28030**
Alpine Invoice Number: **6444**

Auditor Notes:
√ - *tied amounts to product invoice and to the shipping invoices.*

PRODUCT INVOICE

Alpine Cupcakes, Inc.
1250 16th Street
Denver, Colorado 80202

Shipped To:

Country Barrel Restaurant
1400 Poplar Street
Denver, CO 80224

Customer PO: 908
Customer PO Date: 12/01/20X2

Page 1/4
Invoice Number: 6444
Date: 12/31/20X2
Due Date: 1/30/20X3
Sales Order No: 2767

No. Ordered	Date Shipped	No. Shipped	No. Left in Order	Description	Price	Total
352	12/2/20X2	44 √	308	Carrot Cake	$2.40	$105.60
670	12/2/20X2	84	586	Chocolate	$2.40	$201.60
211	12/2/20X2	26	185	Gluten-free Choc.	$2.40	$62.40
458	12/2/20X2	57	401	Lemon	$2.40	$136.80
246	12/2/20X2	31	215	Red Velvet	$2.40	$74.40
246	12/2/20X2	31	215	Spice	$2.40	$74.40
1234	12/2/20X2	154	1080	Vanilla	$2.40	$369.60
105	12/2/20X2	13	92	Almond Vegan	$2.40	$31.20
				Shipment Total		**$1,056.00**
352	12/6/20X2	44	264	Carrot Cake	$2.40	$105.60
670	12/6/20X2	84	502	Chocolate	$2.40	$201.60
211	12/6/20X2	26	159	Gluten-free Choc.	$2.40	$62.40
458	12/6/20X2	57	344	Lemon	$2.40	$136.80
246	12/6/20X2	31	184	Red Velvet	$2.40	$74.40
246	12/6/20X2	31	184	Spice	$2.40	$74.40
1234	12/6/20X2	154	926	Vanilla	$2.40	$369.60
105	12/6/20X2	13	79	Almond Vegan	$2.40	$31.20
				Shipment Total		**$1,056.00**
352	12/10/20X2	44	220	Carrot Cake	$2.40	$105.60
670	12/10/20X2	84	418	Chocolate	$2.40	$201.60
211	12/10/20X2	26	133	Gluten-free Choc.	$2.40	$62.40
458	12/10/20X2	57	287	Lemon	$2.40	$136.80
246	12/10/20X2	31	153	Red Velvet	$2.40	$74.40
246	12/10/20X2	31	153	Spice	$2.40	$74.40
1234	12/10/20X2	154	772	Vanilla	$2.40	$369.60
105	12/10/20X2	13 √	66	Almond Vegan	$2.40	$31.20
				Shipment Total		**$1,056.00**

Client Supporting Document

AR.6.4: pg. 2 of 11

Performed by:
TES 02/13/20X3
Reviewed by:
SDM 2/15/20x3

PRODUCT INVOICE (continued)

Alpine Cupcakes, Inc.
1250 16th Street
Denver, Colorado 80202

Page 2/4

Shipped To:

Country Barrel Restaurant
1400 Poplar Street
Denver, CO 80224

Invoice Number: 6444

Date: 12/31/20X2

Ordered	Date Shipped	No. Shipped	No. Left in Order	Description	Price	Total
352	12/13/20X2	44	176	Carrot Cake	$2.40	$105.60
670	12/13/20X2	84	334	Chocolate	$2.40	$201.60
211	12/13/20X2	26	107	Gluten-free Choc.	$2.40	$62.40
458	12/13/20X2	57	230	Lemon	$2.40	$136.80
246	12/13/20X2	31	122	Red Velvet	$2.40	$74.40
246	12/13/20X2	31	122	Spice	$2.40	$74.40
1234	12/13/20X2	154	618	Vanilla	$2.40	$369.60
105	12/13/20X2	13	53	Almond Vegan	$2.40	$31.20
				Shipment Total		**$1,056.00**
352	12/17/20X2	44	132	Carrot Cake	$2.40	$105.60
670	12/17/20X2	84	250	Chocolate	$2.40	$201.60
211	12/17/20X2	26	81	Gluten-free Choc.	$2.40	$62.40
458	12/17/20X2	57	173	Lemon	$2.40	$136.80
246	12/17/20X2	31	91	Red Velvet	$2.40	$74.40
246	12/17/20X2	31	91	Spice	$2.40	$74.40
1234	12/17/20X2	154	464	Vanilla	$2.40	$369.60
105	12/17/20X2	13	40	Almond Vegan	$2.40	$31.20
				Shipment Total		**$1,056.00**
352	12/22/20X2	44	88	Carrot Cake	$2.40	$105.60
670	12/22/20X2	84	166	Chocolate	$2.40	$201.60
211	12/22/20X2	26	55	Gluten-free Choc.	$2.40	$62.40
458	12/22/20X2	57	116	Lemon	$2.40	$136.80
246	12/22/20X2	31	60	Red Velvet	$2.40	$74.40
246	12/22/20X2	31	60	Spice	$2.40	$74.40
1234	12/22/20X2	154	310	Vanilla	$2.40	$369.60
105	12/22/20X2	13	27	Almond Vegan	$2.40	$31.20
				Shipment Total		**$1,056.00**

Performed by:
TES 02/13/20X3
Reviewed by:
SDM 2/15/20X3

PRODUCT INVOICE (continued)

Alpine Cupcakes, Inc.
1250 16th Street
Denver, Colorado 80202

Page 3/4

Shipped To:

Invoice Number: 6444

Country Barrel Restaurant

Date: 12/31/20X2

1400 Poplar Street

Denver, CO 80224

Ordered	Date Shipped	No. Shipped	No. Left in Order	Description	Price	Total
352	12/26/20X2	44	44	Carrot Cake	$2.40	$105.60
670	12/26/20X2	84	82	Chocolate	$2.40	$201.60
211	12/26/20X2	26	29	Gluten-free Choc.	$2.40	$62.40
458	12/26/20X2	57	59	Lemon	$2.40	$136.80
246	12/26/20X2	31	29	Red Velvet	$2.40	$74.40
246	12/26/20X2	31	29	Spice	$2.40	$74.40
1234	12/26/20X2	154	156	Vanilla	$2.40	$369.60
105	12/26/20X2	13	14	Almond Vegan	$2.40	$31.20
				Shipment Total		**$1,056.00**
352	12/28/20X2	44	0	Carrot Cake	$2.40	$105.60
670	12/28/20X2	82	0	Chocolate	$2.40	$196.80
211	12/28/20X2	29	0	Gluten-free Choc.	$2.40	$69.60
458	12/28/20X2	59	0	Lemon	$2.40	$141.60
246	12/28/20X2	29	0	Red Velvet	$2.40	$69.60
246	12/28/20X2	29	0	Spice	$2.40	$69.60
1234	12/28/20X2	156	0	Vanilla	$2.40	$374.40
105	12/28/20X2	14	0	Almond Vegan	$2.40	$33.60
				Shipment Total		**$1,060.80**

Sales Tax	N/A
Freight	N/A
Invoice Total	$8,452.80

AR.6.1

Performed by:
TES 02/13/20X3
Reviewed by:
SDM 2/15/20x3

Please return this page with your payment

PRODUCT INVOICE

Remittance Advice   Page 4/4
Country Barrel
Restaurant   Invoice Number: 6444
1400 Poplar Street   Sales Order No: 2767
Denver, CO 80224   Customer PO: 908
                                    Customer PO Date: 12/01/20X2
                                    Total Amount Owed: $8,452.80
                                    Date Due: 1/30/20X3

Date Paid   _____

Amount Paid   _____

Pmt Received
1/27/20X3

Lindsay McKenna

See returned remittance form

Auditor Notes:

Calculated totals and tied amounts to customer purchase order and shipping invoice.

Carrot Cake = 352 √	*Red Velvet = 246* √
Chocolate = 670 √	*Spice = 246* √
Gluten-free Chocolate = 211 √	*Vanilla = 1,234* √
Lemon = 458 √	*Almond Vegan = 105* √

Alpine Cupcakes, Inc.
Sales Cutoff Testing
Country Barrel Before Year End

Performed by:
TES 02/13/20X3
Reviewed by:
SDM 2/15/20x3

SHIPPING INVOICE

Alpine Cupcakes, Inc.
1250 16th Street
Denver, Colorado 80202

Page 1/4

Shipped To:

Country Barrel Restaurant

1400 Poplar Street, Denver, CO 80224

Customer PO: 908   Customer PO Date: 12/1/20X2

Ship Invoice Number: S6444

Date: 12/31/20X2

Due Date: 1/30/20X3

Sales Order No: 2767

Shipping Report # 27731

No. Ordered	Date Shipped		Dozen Shipped	Description	Price per Dozen	Total
352	12/2/20X2	√	3.67	Carrot Cake	$0.20	$0.73
670	12/2/20X2		7.00	Chocolate	$0.20	$1.40
211	12/2/20X2		2.17	Gluten-free Choc.	$0.20	$0.43
458	12/2/20X2		4.75	Lemon	$0.20	$0.95
246	12/2/20X2		2.58	Red Velvet	$0.20	$0.52
246	12/2/20X2		2.58	Spice	$0.20	$0.52
1234	12/2/20X2		12.83	Vanilla	$0.20	$2.57
105	12/2/20X2		1.08	Almond Vegan	$0.20	$0.22
	Total Shipped		**36.66**	**Price per Dozen**	**$0.20**	**$7.33**

Shipping Report # 27762

No. Ordered	Date Shipped	Dozen Shipped	Description	Price per Dozen	Total
352	12/6/20X2	3.67	Carrot Cake	$0.20	$0.73
670	12/6/20X2	7.00	Chocolate	$0.20	$1.40
211	12/6/20X2	2.17	Gluten-free Choc.	$0.20	$0.43
458	12/6/20X2	4.75	Lemon	$0.20	$0.95
246	12/6/20X2	2.58	Red Velvet	$0.20	$0.52
246	12/6/20X2	2.58	Spice	$0.20	$0.52
1234	12/6/20X2	12.83	Vanilla	$0.20	$2.57
105	12/6/20X2	1.08	Almond Vegan	$0.20	$0.22
	Total Shipped	**36.66**	**Price per Dozen**	**$0.20**	**$7.33**

Shipping Report # 27801

No. Ordered	Date Shipped		Dozen Shipped	Description	Price per Dozen	Total
352	12/10/20X2		3.67	Carrot Cake	$0.20	$0.73
670	12/10/20X2		7.00	Chocolate	$0.20	$1.40
211	12/10/20X2		2.17	Gluten-free Choc.	$0.20	$0.43
458	12/10/20X2		4.75	Lemon	$0.20	$0.95
246	12/10/20X2		2.58	Red Velvet	$0.20	$0.52
246	12/10/20X2		2.58	Spice	$0.20	$0.52
1234	12/10/20X2		12.83	Vanilla	$0.20	$2.57
105	12/10/20X2		1.08	Almond Vegan	$0.20	$0.22
	Total Shipped	√	**36.66**	**Price per Dozen**	**$0.20**	**$7.33**

Client Supporting Document

AR.6.4: pg. 6 of 11

Performed by:
TES 02/13/20X3
Reviewed by:
SDM 2/15/20x3

SHIPPING INVOICE (continued)

Alpine Cupcakes, Inc.
1250 16th Street
Denver, Colorado 80202

Page 2/4

Shipped To:

Country Barrel Restaurant

1400 Poplar Street, Denver, CO 80224

Ship Invoice Number: S6444

Date: 12/31/20X2

Shipping Report # 27827

Ordered	Date Shipped		Dozen Shipped	Description	Price per Dozen	Total
352	12/13/20X2	√	3.67	Carrot Cake	$0.20	$0.73
670	12/13/20X2		7.00	Chocolate	$0.20	$1.40
211	12/13/20X2		2.17	Gluten-free Choc.	$0.20	$0.43
458	12/13/20X2		4.75	Lemon	$0.20	$0.95
246	12/13/20X2		2.58	Red Velvet	$0.20	$0.52
246	12/13/20X2		2.58	Spice	$0.20	$0.52
1234	12/13/20X2		12.83	Vanilla	$0.20	$2.57
105	12/13/20X2		1.08	Almond Vegan	$0.20	$0.22
	Total Shipped		**36.66**	**Price per Dozen**	**$0.20**	**$7.33**

Shipping Report # 27840

Ordered	Date Shipped	Dozen Shipped	Description	Price per Dozen	Total
352	12/17/20X2	3.67	Carrot Cake	$0.20	$0.73
670	12/17/20X2	7.00	Chocolate	$0.20	$1.40
211	12/17/20X2	2.17	Gluten-free Choc.	$0.20	$0.43
458	12/17/20X2	4.75	Lemon	$0.20	$0.95
246	12/17/20X2	2.58	Red Velvet	$0.20	$0.52
246	12/17/20X2	2.58	Spice	$0.20	$0.52
1234	12/17/20X2	12.83	Vanilla	$0.20	$2.57
105	12/17/20X2	1.08	Almond Vegan	$0.20	$0.22
	Total Shipped	**36.66**	**Price per Dozen**	**$0.20**	**$7.33**

Shipping Report # 27852

Ordered	Date Shipped	Dozen Shipped	Description	Price per Dozen	Total
352	12/22/20X2	3.67	Carrot Cake	$0.20	$0.73
670	12/22/20X2	7.00	Chocolate	$0.20	$1.40
211	12/22/20X2	2.17	Gluten-free Choc.	$0.20	$0.43
458	12/22/20X2	4.75	Lemon	$0.20	$0.95
246	12/22/20X2	2.58	Red Velvet	$0.20	$0.52
246	12/22/20X2	2.58	Spice	$0.20	$0.52
1234	12/22/20X2	12.83	Vanilla	$0.20	$2.57
105	12/22/20X2	1.08	Almond Vegan	$0.20	$0.22
	Total Shipped √	**36.66**	**Price per Dozen**	**$0.20**	**$7.33**

SHIPPING INVOICE (continued)

Alpine Cupcakes, Inc.
1250 16th Street
Denver, Colorado 80202

Page 3/4

Shipped To:

Country Barrel Restaurant

1400 Poplar Street

Denver, CO 80224

Ship Invoice Number: S6444

Date: 12/31/20X2

Shipping Report # 27954

Ordered	Date Shipped	Dozen Shipped	Description	Price per Dozen	Total
352	12/26/20X2	√ 3.67 µ	Carrot Cake	$0.20	$0.73
670	12/26/20X2	7.00	Chocolate	$0.20	$1.40
211	12/26/20X2	2.17	Gluten-free Choc.	$0.20	$0.43
458	12/26/20X2	4.75	Lemon	$0.20	$0.95
246	12/26/20X2	2.58	Red Velvet	$0.20	$0.52
246	12/26/20X2	2.58	Spice	$0.20	$0.52
1234	12/26/20X2	12.83	Vanilla	$0.20	$2.57
105	12/26/20X2	1.08	Almond Vegan	$0.20	$0.22
	Total Shipped	**36.66**	**Price per Dozen**	**$0.20**	**$7.33**

Shipping Report # 28030

Ordered	Date Shipped	Dozen Shipped	Description	Price per Dozen	Total
352	12/28/20X2	3.67	Carrot Cake	$0.20	$0.73
670	12/28/20X2	6.83	Chocolate	$0.20	$1.37
211	12/28/20X2	2.42	Gluten-free Choc.	$0.20	$0.48
458	12/28/20X2	4.92	Lemon	$0.20	$0.98
246	12/28/20X2	2.42	Red Velvet	$0.20	$0.48
246	12/28/20X2	2.42	Spice	$0.20	$0.48
1234	12/28/20X2	13.00	Vanilla	$0.20	$2.60
105	12/28/20X2	1.17	Almond Vegan	$0.20	$0.23
	Total Shipped	**36.85**	**Price per Dozen**	**$0.20**	**$7.37**

Sales Tax		N/A
Invoice Total		$58.70

Performed by:
TES 02/13/20X3
Reviewed by:
SDM 2/15/20x3

Please return this page with your payment

SHIPPING INVOICE

Remittance Advice   Page 4/4

Country Barrel Restaurant   Invoice Number: S6444
1400 Poplar Street   Sales Order No: 2767
Denver, CO 80224   Customer PO: 908
                                   Customer PO Date: 12/01/20X2
                                   Amount Due: $58.70
                                   Date Due: 1/30/20X3

Date Paid _____

Amount Paid _____

Pmt Received 1/29/20X3

Lindsay McKenna

See returned remittance form

Auditor Notes:

Sum of Items Shipped: Calculated totals by adding up the Dozen Shipped per cupcake type and then multiplying by 12.
Tied totals per cupcake type to customer purchase order and product invoice.

Carrot Cake = 29.36 * 12 = 352 √   *Red Velvet = 20.48 * 12 = 246* √

Chocolate = 55.83 * 12 = 670 √   *Spice = 20.48 * 12 = 246* √

Gluten-free Chocolate = 17.61 * 12 = 211 √   *Vanilla = 102.81 * 12 = 1,234* √

Lemon = 38.17 * 12 = 458 √   *Almond Vegan = 8.73 * 12 = 105* √

Calculated totals of items shipped 5 days before year end by adding up the dozens of items shipped by cupcake type
multiplied by 12. Amounts were tied to the shipping reports.

Carrot Cake = 7.34 * 12 = 88 μ   *Red Velvet = 5.00 * 12 = 60* μ

Chocolate = 13.83 * 12 = 166 μ   *Spice = 5.00 * 12 = 60* μ

Gluten-free Chocolate = 4.59 * 12 = 55 μ   *Vanilla = 25.83 * 12 = 310* μ

Lemon = 9.67 * 12 = 116 μ   *Almond Vegan = 2.25 * 12 = 27* μ

Performed by:
TES 02/13/20X3
Reviewed by:
SDM 2/15/20x3

ALPINE CUPCAKES, INC.
Shipping Report

Date: 12/22/20X2

Purchase Order #: 908   **Shipping Report # 27852**

Shipped To: Country Barrel Restaurants

Freight Carrier: Alpine Cupcake Carrier

Quantity		Unit	Description
44	μ	Cupcakes	Carrot Cake
84		Cupcakes	Chocolate
26		Cupcakes	Gluten-free Chocolate
57		Cupcakes	Lemon
31		Cupcakes	Red Velvet
31		Cupcakes	Spice
154		Cupcakes	Vanilla
13		Cupcakes	Almond Vegan

Remarks: Items received in OK condition

Received By: Will Temple

Delivered To: Receiving Dept.

ALPINE CUPCAKES, INC.
Shipping Report

Date: 12/26/20X2

Purchase Order #: 908   **Shipping Report # 27954**

Shipped To: Country Barrel Restaurants

Freight Carrier: Alpine Cupcake Carrier

Quantity		Unit	Description
44	μ	Cupcakes	Carrot Cake
84		Cupcakes	Chocolate
26		Cupcakes	Gluten-free Chocolate
57		Cupcakes	Lemon
31		Cupcakes	Red Velvet
31		Cupcakes	Spice
154		Cupcakes	Vanilla
13		Cupcakes	Almond Vegan

Remarks: Items received in OK condition

Received By: Will Temple

Delivered To: Receiving Dept.

Alpine Cupcakes, Inc.
Sales Cutoff Testing
Country Barrel Before Year End

Performed by:
TES 02/13/20X3
Reviewed by:
SDM 2/15/20x3

ALPINE CUPCAKES, INC.
Shipping Report

Date: 12/28/20X2
Purchase Order #: 908   **Shipping Report # 28030**
Shipped To: Country Barrel Restaurants
Freight Carrier: Alpine Cupcake Carrier

Quantity	Unit	Description
44 μ	Cupcakes	Carrot Cake
82	Cupcakes	Chocolate
29	Cupcakes	Gluten-free Chocolate
59	Cupcakes	Lemon
29	Cupcakes	Red Velvet
29	Cupcakes	Spice
156	Cupcakes	Vanilla
14	Cupcakes	Almond Vegan

Remarks: Items received in OK condition
Received By: Will Temple
Delivered To: Receiving Dept.

Auditor Notes:

Calculated totals of items shipped 5 days before year end by adding up the number of items shipped by cupcake type. Amounts were tied to the shipping invoice.

Carrot Cake = 132 μ   Red Velvet = 91 μ
Chocolate = 250 μ   Spice = 91 μ
Gluten-free Chocolate = 81 μ   Vanilla = 464 μ
Lemon = 173 μ   Almond Vegan = 40 μ

Performed by:
TES 02/13/20X3
Reviewed by:
SDM 2/15/20x3

PRODUCT INVOICE

Alpine Cupcakes, Inc.
1250 16th Street
Denver, Colorado 80202

Page 1/4

Shipped To:

Country Barrel Restaurant
1400 Poplar Street
Denver, CO 80224

Customer PO: 922
Customer PO Date: 1/03/20X3

Invoice Number: 6477
Date: 1/31/20X3
Due Date: 3/1/20X3
Sales Order No: 2800

No. Ordered	Date Shipped	No. Shipped	No. Left in Order	Description	Price	Total
393	1/04/20X3	49	344	Carrot Cake	$2.40	$117.60
645	1/04/20X3	81	564	Chocolate	$2.40	$194.40
280	1/04/20X3	35	245	Gluten-free Choc.	$2.40	$84.00
336	1/04/20X3	42	294	Lemon	$2.40	$100.80
252	1/04/20X3	32	220	Red Velvet	$2.40	$76.80
308	1/04/20X3	39	269	Spice	$2.40	$93.60
533	1/04/20X3	67	466	Vanilla	$2.40	$160.80
56	1/04/20X3	7	49	Almond Vegan	$2.40	$16.80
				Shipment Total		**$844.80**
393	1/07/20X3	49	295	Carrot Cake	$2.40	$117.60
645	1/07/20X3	81	483	Chocolate	$2.40	$194.40
280	1/07/20X3	35	210	Gluten-free Choc.	$2.40	$84.00
336	1/07/20X3	42	252	Lemon	$2.40	$100.80
252	1/07/20X3	32	188	Red Velvet	$2.40	$76.80
308	1/07/20X3	39	230	Spice	$2.40	$93.60
533	1/07/20X3	67	399	Vanilla	$2.40	$160.80
56	1/07/20X3	7	42	Almond Vegan	$2.40	$16.80
				Shipment Total		**$844.80**
393	1/12/20X3	49	246	Carrot Cake	$2.40	$117.60
645	1/12/20X3	81	402	Chocolate	$2.40	$194.40
280	1/12/20X3	35	175	Gluten-free Choc.	$2.40	$84.00
336	1/12/20X3	42	210	Lemon	$2.40	$100.80
252	1/12/20X3	32	156	Red Velvet	$2.40	$76.80
308	1/12/20X3	39	191	Spice	$2.40	$93.60
533	1/12/20X3	67	332	Vanilla	$2.40	$160.80
56	1/12/20X3	7	35	Almond Vegan	$2.40	$16.80
				Shipment Total		**$844.80**

Client Supporting Document

AR.6.5: pg. 1 of 8

Performed by:
TES 02/13/20X3
Reviewed by:
SDM 2/15/20x3

PRODUCT INVOICE (continued)

Alpine Cupcakes, Inc.
1250 16th Street
Denver, Colorado 80202

Page 2/4

Shipped To:

Invoice Number: 6477

Country Barrel Restaurant

Date: 1/31/20X3

1400 Poplar Street

Denver, CO 80224

Ordered	Date Shipped	No. Shipped		No. Left in Order	Description	Price	Total
393	1/16/20X3	49	√	197	Carrot Cake	$2.40	$117.60
645	1/16/20X3	81		321	Chocolate	$2.40	$194.40
280	1/16/20X3	35		140	Gluten-free Choc.	$2.40	$84.00
336	1/16/20X3	42		168	Lemon	$2.40	$100.80
252	1/16/20X3	32		124	Red Velvet	$2.40	$76.80
308	1/16/20X3	39		152	Spice	$2.40	$93.60
533	1/16/20X3	67		265	Vanilla	$2.40	$160.80
56	1/16/20X3	7		28	Almond Vegan	$2.40	$16.80
					Shipment Total		**$844.80**
393	1/20/20X3	49		148	Carrot Cake	$2.40	$117.60
645	1/20/20X3	81		240	Chocolate	$2.40	$194.40
280	1/20/20X3	35		105	Gluten-free Choc.	$2.40	$84.00
336	1/20/20X3	42		126	Lemon	$2.40	$100.80
252	1/20/20X3	32		92	Red Velvet	$2.40	$76.80
308	1/20/20X3	39		113	Spice	$2.40	$93.60
533	1/20/20X3	67		198	Vanilla	$2.40	$160.80
56	1/20/20X3	7		21	Almond Vegan	$2.40	$16.80
					Shipment Total		**$844.80**
393	1/24/20X3	49		99	Carrot Cake	$2.40	$117.60
645	1/24/20X3	81		159	Chocolate	$2.40	$194.40
280	1/24/20X3	35		70	Gluten-free Choc.	$2.40	$84.00
336	1/24/20X3	42		84	Lemon	$2.40	$100.80
252	1/24/20X3	32		60	Red Velvet	$2.40	$76.80
308	1/24/20X3	39		74	Spice	$2.40	$93.60
533	1/24/20X3	67		131	Vanilla	$2.40	$160.80
56	1/24/20X3	7	↓	14	Almond Vegan	$2.40	$16.80
					Shipment Total		**$844.80**

Performed by:
TES 02/13/20X3
Reviewed by:
SDM 2/15/20x3

PRODUCT INVOICE (continued)

Alpine Cupcakes, Inc.
1250 16th Street
Denver, Colorado 80202

Page 3/4

Shipped To:

Country Barrel Restaurant
1400 Poplar Street
Denver, CO 80224

Invoice Number: 6477
Date: 1/31/20X3

Ordered	Date Shipped	No. Shipped	No. Left in Order	Description	Price	Total
393	1/29/20X3	49 √	50	Carrot Cake	$2.40	$117.60
645	1/29/20X3	81	78	Chocolate	$2.40	$194.40
280	1/29/20X3	35	35	Gluten-free Choc.	$2.40	$84.00
336	1/29/20X3	42	42	Lemon	$2.40	$100.80
252	1/29/20X3	32	28	Red Velvet	$2.40	$76.80
308	1/29/20X3	39	35	Spice	$2.40	$93.60
533	1/29/20X3	67	64	Vanilla	$2.40	$160.80
56	1/29/20X3	7	7	Almond Vegan	$2.40	$16.80
				Shipment Total		**$844.80**
393	1/31/20X3	50	0	Carrot Cake	$2.40	$120.00
645	1/31/20X3	78	0	Chocolate	$2.40	$187.20
280	1/31/20X3	35	0	Gluten-free Choc.	$2.40	$84.00
336	1/31/20X3	42	0	Lemon	$2.40	$100.80
252	1/31/20X3	28	0	Red Velvet	$2.40	$67.20
308	1/31/20X3	35	0	Spice	$2.40	$84.00
533	1/31/20X3	64	0	Vanilla	$2.40	$153.60
56	1/31/20X3	7	0	Almond Vegan	$2.40	$16.80
				Shipment Total		**$813.60**

Sales Tax		N/A
Freight		N/A
Invoice Total		$6,727. 20

AR.6.1

Client Supporting Document

Alpine Cupcakes, Inc.
Sales Cutoff Testing
Country Barrel After Year End

Please return this page with your payment

PRODUCT INVOICE

Remittance Advice   Page 4/4

Country Barrel Restaurant   Invoice Number: 6477
1400 Poplar Street   Sales Order No: 2800
Denver, CO 80224   Customer PO: 922
                                 Customer PO Date: 1/03/20X3
                                 Total Amount Owed: $6,727.20
                                 Date Due: 3/01/20X3

Date Paid   _____

Amount Paid   _____

Pmt Received
3/05/20X3

Lindsay McKenna

See returned remittance form

Auditor Notes:
Calculated totals and tied amounts to customer purchase order and shipping invoice.

Carrot Cake = 393 √	*Red Velvet* = 252 √
Chocolate = 645 √	*Spice* = 308 √
Gluten-free Chocolate = 280 √	*Vanilla* = 533 √
Lemon = 336 √	*Almond Vegan* = 56 √

Alpine Cupcakes, Inc.
Sales Cutoff Testing
Country Barrel After Year End

Performed by:
TES 02/13/20X3
Reviewed by:
SDM 2/15/20x3

SHIPPING INVOICE

Alpine Cupcakes, Inc.
1250 16th Street
Denver, Colorado 80202

Shipped To:

Country Barrel Restaurant

1400 Poplar Street, Denver, CO 80224

Customer PO: 922   Customer PO Date: 1/03/20X3

Ship Invoice Number: S6477

Date: 1/31/20X3

Due Date: 3/02/20X3

Sales Order No: 2800

Shipping Report # 28047

No. Ordered	Date Shipped	Dozen Shipped	Description	Price per Dozen	Total
393	1/04/20X3 √	4.08 μ	Carrot Cake	$0.20	$0.82
645	1/04/20X3	6.75	Chocolate	$0.20	$1.35
280	1/04/20X3	2.92	Gluten-free Choc.	$0.20	$0.58
336	1/04/20X3	3.50	Lemon	$0.20	$0.70
252	1/04/20X3	2.67	Red Velvet	$0.20	$0.53
308	1/04/20X3	3.25	Spice	$0.20	$0.65
533	1/04/20X3	5.58	Vanilla	$0.20	$1.12
56	1/04/20X3	0.58	Almond Vegan	$0.20	$0.12
Total Shipped		**29.33**	**Price per Dozen**	**$0.20**	**$5.87**

Shipping Report # 28132

No. Ordered	Date Shipped	Dozen Shipped	Description	Price per Dozen	Total
393	1/07/20X3	4.08	Carrot Cake	$0.20	$0.82
645	1/07/20X3	6.75	Chocolate	$0.20	$1.35
280	1/07/20X3	2.92	Gluten-free Choc.	$0.20	$0.58
336	1/07/20X3	3.50	Lemon	$0.20	$0.70
252	1/07/20X3	2.67	Red Velvet	$0.20	$0.53
308	1/07/20X3	3.25	Spice	$0.20	$0.65
533	1/07/20X3	5.58	Vanilla	$0.20	$1.12
56	1/07/20X3	0.58	Almond Vegan	$0.20	$0.12
Total Shipped		**29.33**	**Price per Dozen**	**$0.20**	**$5.87**

Shipping Report # 28176

No. Ordered	Date Shipped	Dozen Shipped	Description	Price per Dozen	Total
393	1/12/20X3	4.08	Carrot Cake	$0.20	$0.82
645	1/12/20X3	6.75	Chocolate	$0.20	$1.35
280	1/12/20X3	2.92	Gluten-free Choc.	$0.20	$0.58
336	1/12/20X3	3.50	Lemon	$0.20	$0.70
252	1/12/20X3	2.67	Red Velvet	$0.20	$0.53
308	1/12/20X3	3.25	Spice	$0.20	$0.65
533	1/12/20X3	5.58	Vanilla	$0.20	$1.12
56	1/12/20X3	0.58	Almond Vegan	$0.20	$0.12
Total Shipped		**29.33**	**Price per Dozen**	**$0.20**	**$5.87**

Client Supporting Document

AR.6.5: pg. 5 of 8

| Performed by: |
| *TES 02/13/20X3* |
| Reviewed by: |
| SDM 2/15/20x3 |

SHIPPING INVOICE (continued)

Alpine Cupcakes, Inc.
1250 16th Street
Denver, Colorado 80202

Page 2/4
Ship Invoice Number:
S6477

Date: 1/31/20X3

Shipped To:

Country Barrel Restaurant

1400 Poplar Street, Denver, CO 80224

Shipping Report # 28199

Ordered	Date Shipped	Dozen Shipped	Description	Price per Dozen	Total
393	1/16/20X3 ✓	4.08	Carrot Cake	$0.20	$0.82
645	1/16/20X3	6.75	Chocolate	$0.20	$1.35
280	1/16/20X3	2.92	Gluten-free Choc.	$0.20	$0.58
336	1/16/20X3	3.50	Lemon	$0.20	$0.70
252	1/16/20X3	2.67	Red Velvet	$0.20	$0.53
308	1/16/20X3	3.25	Spice	$0.20	$0.65
533	1/16/20X3	5.58	Vanilla	$0.20	$1.12
56	1/16/20X3	0.58	Almond Vegan	$0.20	$0.12
	Total Shipped	**29.33**	**Price per Dozen**	**$0.20**	**$5.87**

Shipping Report # 29221

Ordered	Date Shipped	Dozen Shipped	Description	Price per Dozen	Total
393	1/20/20X3	4.08	Carrot Cake	$0.20	$0.82
645	1/20/20X3	6.75	Chocolate	$0.20	$1.35
280	1/20/20X3	2.92	Gluten-free Choc.	$0.20	$0.58
336	1/20/20X3	3.50	Lemon	$0.20	$0.70
252	1/20/20X3	2.67	Red Velvet	$0.20	$0.53
308	1/20/20X3	3.25	Spice	$0.20	$0.65
533	1/20/20X3	5.58	Vanilla	$0.20	$1.12
56	1/20/20X3	0.58	Almond Vegan	$0.20	$0.12
	Total Shipped	**29.33**	**Price per Dozen**	**$0.20**	**$5.87**

Shipping Report # 28273

Ordered	Date Shipped	Dozen Shipped	Description	Price per Dozen	Total
393	1/24/20X3	4.08	Carrot Cake	$0.20	$0.82
645	1/24/20X3	6.75	Chocolate	$0.20	$1.35
280	1/24/20X3	2.92	Gluten-free Choc.	$0.20	$0.58
336	1/24/20X3	3.50	Lemon	$0.20	$0.70
252	1/24/20X3	2.67	Red Velvet	$0.20	$0.53
308	1/24/20X3	3.25	Spice	$0.20	$0.65
533	1/24/20X3	5.58	Vanilla	$0.20	$1.12
56	1/24/20X3	0.58	Almond Vegan	$0.20	$0.12
	Total Shipped ✓	**29.33**	**Price per Dozen**	**$0.20**	**$5.87**

Performed by:
TES 02/13/20X3
Reviewed by:
SDM 2/15/20x3

SHIPPING INVOICE (continued)

Alpine Cupcakes, Inc.
1250 16th Street
Denver, Colorado 80202

Page 3/4

Shipped To:

Country Barrel Restaurant

1400 Poplar Street, Denver, CO 80224

Ship Invoice Number: S6477

Date: 1/31/20X3

Shipping Report # 28305

Ordered	Date Shipped		Dozen Shipped	Description	Price per Dozen	Total
393	1/29/20X3	√	4.08	Carrot Cake	$0.20	$0.82
645	1/29/20X3		6.75	Chocolate	$0.20	$1.35
280	1/29/20X3		2.92	Gluten-free Choc.	$0.20	$0.58
336	1/29/20X3		3.50	Lemon	$0.20	$0.70
252	1/29/20X3		2.67	Red Velvet	$0.20	$0.53
308	1/29/20X3		3.25	Spice	$0.20	$0.65
533	1/29/20X3		5.58	Vanilla	$0.20	$1.12
56	1/29/20X3		0.58	Almond Vegan	$0.20	$0.12
Total Shipped			**29.33**	**Price per Dozen**	**$0.20**	**$5.87**

Shipping Report # 28334

Ordered	Date Shipped		Dozen Shipped	Description	Price per Dozen	Total
393	1/31/20X3		4.17	Carrot Cake	$0.20	$0.83
645	1/31/20X3		6.50	Chocolate	$0.20	$1.30
280	1/31/20X3		2.92	Gluten-free Choc.	$0.20	$0.58
336	1/31/20X3		3.50	Lemon	$0.20	$0.70
252	1/31/20X3		2.33	Red Velvet	$0.20	$0.47
308	1/31/20X3		2.92	Spice	$0.20	$0.58
533	1/31/20X3		5.33	Vanilla	$0.20	$1.07
56	1/31/20X3		0.58	Almond Vegan	$0.20	$0.12
Total Shipped		√	**28.25**	**Price per Dozen**	**$0.20**	**$5.65**

Sales Tax	N/A
Invoice Total	$46.72

| Performed by: |
| TES 02/13/20X3 |
| Reviewed by: |
| SDM 2/15/20X3 |

Please return this page with your payment

SHIPPING INVOICE

Remittance Advice
Country Barrel Restaurant
1400 Poplar Street
Denver, CO 80224

Page 4/4

Invoice Number:	S6477
Sales Order No:	2800
Customer PO:	922
Customer PO Date:	1/03/20X3
Amount Due:	$46.72
Date Due:	3/02/20X3

Date Paid _____

Amount Paid _____

**Pmt Received
3/04/20X3**

Lindsay McKenna

See returned remittance form

Auditor Notes:

Sum of Items Shipped: Calculated totals by adding up the Dozen Shipped per cupcake type and then multiplying by 12. Tied totals per cupcake type to customer purchase order and product invoice.

*Carrot Cake = 32.73 * 12 = 393   √*   *Red Velvet = 21.02 * 12 = 252   √*

*Chocolate = 53.75 * 12 = 645   √*   *Spice = 25.67 * 12 = 308   √*

*Gluten-free Chocolate = 23.36 * 12 = 280   √*   *Vanilla = 44.39 * 12 = 533   √*

*Lemon = 28.0 * 12 = 336   √*   *Almond Vegan = 4.64 * 12 = 56   √*

Calculated totals of items shipped 5 days after year end by adding up the dozens of items shipped by cupcake type multiplied by 12. Amounts were tied to the shipping reports.

*Carrot Cake = 4.08 * 12 = 49   µ*   *Red Velvet = 2.67 * 12 = 32   µ*

*Chocolate = 6.75 * 12 = 81   µ*   *Spice = 3.25 * 12 = 39   µ*

*Gluten-free Chocolate = 2.92 * 12 = 35   µ*   *Vanilla = 5.58 * 12 = 67   µ*

*Lemon = 3.50 * 12 = 42   µ*   *Almond Vegan = 0.58 * 12 = 7   µ*

Client Supporting Document

AR.6.5: pg. 8 of 8

Alpine Cupcakes, Inc.
Sales Journal
December 20X2

Performed by:

Reviewed by:

	Deliveries per Month	Sales Date	Carrot Cake	Chocolate	Gluten-free Chocolate	Lemon	Red Velvet	Spice	Vanilla	Vegan	Total Order	Invoice Total	
Bon Appetito Restaurants	12	12/31/20X2	707	1343	424	919	495	495	2475	212	7070	$16,968.00	
Boulder Tea House	8	12/31/20X2	24	46	14	31	17	17	85	7	241	$578.40	
Broken Eggs Restaurant	12	12/31/20X2	90	171	54	117	63	63	316	27	901	$2,162.40	
Brown's Tavern	8	12/31/20X2	19	36	11	24	13	13	66	5	187	$448.80	
Bubba's Fish House	8	12/31/20X2	51	97	30	66	35	35	179	15	508	$1,219.20	
Buckhead Restaurants	8	12/31/20X2	110	209	66	143	77	77	386	33	1101	$2,642.40	
Chavez Cantina	8	12/31/20X2	197	374	118	256	137	137	689	59	1967	$4,720.80	
Country Barrel Restaurants	20	12/31/20X2	352	670	211	458	246	246	1234	105	3522	$8,452.80	AR.6.1
Denver Bakery Café	8	12/31/20X2	241	459	144	314	169	169	845	72	2413	$5,791.20	
Denver Sirloin Restaurants	12	12/31/20X2	194	370	116	253	136	136	681	58	1944	$4,665.60	
Elkhorn Coffee Shops	20	12/31/20X2	436	829	261	567	305	305	1527	130	4360	$10,464.00	
Fontana Catering & Café	3	12/31/20X2	143	272	86	186	100	100	501	43	1431	$3,434.40	
Granny's Café	12	12/31/20X2	156	297	93	203	109	109	547	46	1560	$3,744.00	
High Country Coffee	20	12/31/20X2	242	460	145	314	169	169	848	72	2419	$5,805.60	
Julie's Wraps	8	12/31/20X2	67	128	40	87	47	47	235	20	671	$1,610.40	
Little's Grill	8	12/31/20X2	47	90	28	61	33	33	166	14	472	$1,132.80	
Luigi's Bistro	8	12/31/20X2	62	119	37	81	43	43	219	18	622	$1,492.80	
Mile High Steakhouses	8	12/31/20X2	471	896	283	613	330	330	1650	141	4714	$11,313.60	
Mountain Lion Restaurant	8	12/31/20X2	141	268	84	183	98	98	493	42	1407	$3,376.80	
Mountain Trout Fish House	8	12/31/20X2	143	272	86	186	100	100	501	43	1431	$3,434.40	
Nora's Café	12	12/31/20X2	185	352	111	241	129	129	649	55	1851	$4,442.40	
Papa's Restaurant	4	12/31/20X2	133	253	80	173	93	93	466	40	1331	$3,194.40	
Pebbles Inn	12	12/31/20X2	65	125	39	85	46	46	230	19	655	$1,572.00	
Scotty's Taverns	8	12/31/20X2	95	180	57	123	66	66	332	28	947	$2,272.80	
Smokey's Barbeque Pit	8	12/31/20X2	198	377	119	258	139	139	695	59	1984	$4,761.60	AR.6.1
Southside Café	8	12/31/20X2	54	103	32	70	38	38	190	16	541	$1,298.40	

Client Supporting Document

Alpine Cakes, Inc.
Sales Journal
December 20X2

	Deliveries per Month	Sales Date	Carrot Cake	Chocolate	Gluten-free Chocolate	Lemon	Red Velvet	Spice	Vanilla	Vegan	Total Order	Invoice Total
St. Francis Hotel and Spa	8	12/31/20X2	233	444	140	304	163	163	818	70	2335	$5,604.00
Steinberg Delis	8	12/31/20X2	87	166	52	113	61	61	305	26	871	$2,090.40
The Breakfast Place	12	12/31/20X2	171	326	103	223	120	120	601	51	1715	$4,116.00
The Sandwich Place	8	12/31/20X2	35	66	21	45	24	24	123	10	348	$835.20
UC Boulder Food Service	20	12/31/20X2	611	1161	366	794	427	427	2139	183	6108	$14,659.20
UC Denver Food Service	20	12/31/20X2	474	900	284	616	331	331	1659	142	4737	$11,368.80
												$149,673.60

Client Supporting Document

AR.6.6: pg. 2 of 2

Alpine Cupcakes, Inc.
Sales Journal
January 20X3

Performed by:

Reviewed by:

Name	Deliveries per Month	Sales Date	Carrot Cake	Chocolate	Gluten-free Chocolate	Lemon	Red Velvet	Spice	Vanilla	Vegan	Total Order	Invoice Total
Bon Appetito Restaurants	12	1/31/20X3	631	1036	450	540	405	495	856	90	4503	$10,807.20
Boulder Tea House	8	1/31/20X3	90	148	64	77	58	71	122	12	642	$1,540.80
Broken Eggs Restaurant	12	1/31/20X3	70	115	50	60	45	55	95	10	500	$1,200.00
Brown's Tavern	8	1/31/20X3	72	119	51	62	46	56	98	10	514	$1,233.60
Bubba's Fish House	8	1/31/20X3	164	270	117	141	105	129	223	23	1172	$2,812.80
Buckhead Restaurants	8	1/31/20X3	106	175	76	91	68	83	144	15	758	$1,819.20
Chavez Cantina	8	1/31/20X3	203	333	145	174	130	159	275	29	1448	$3,475.20
Country Barrel Restaurants	20	1/31/20X3	393	645	280	336	252	308	533	56	2803	$6,727.20 *AR.6.1*
Denver Bakery Café	8	1/31/20X3	210	345	150	180	135	165	285	30	1500	$3,600.00
Denver Sirloin Restaurants	12	1/31/20X3	150	246	107	128	96	117	203	21	1068	$2,563.20
Elkhorn Coffee Shops	20	1/31/20X3	380	625	272	326	244	299	516	54	2716	$6,518.40
Fontana Catering & Café	3	1/31/20X3	94	154	67	80	60	74	127	13	669	$1,605.60
Granny's Café	12	1/31/20X3	76	126	54	65	49	60	104	10	544	$1,305.60
High Country Coffee	20	1/31/20X3	213	351	152	183	137	168	290	30	1524	$3,657.60
Julie's Wraps	8	1/31/20X3	144	237	103	123	92	113	195	20	1027	$2,464.80
Little's Grill	8	1/31/20X3	41	67	29	35	26	32	55	5	290	$696.00
Luigi's Bistro	8	1/31/20X3	17	28	12	14	11	13	23	2	120	$288.00
Mile High Steakhouses	8	1/31/20X3	384	631	274	329	247	302	521	54	2742	$6,580.80
Mountain Lion Restaurant	8	1/31/20X3	141	232	101	121	90	111	191	20	1007	$2,416.80
Mountain Trout Fish House	8	1/31/20X3	80	132	57	69	51	63	109	11	572	$1,372.80
Nora's Café	12	1/31/20X3	128	210	91	110	82	100	174	18	913	$2,191.20
Papa's Restaurant	4	1/31/20X3	103	170	74	88	66	81	140	14	736	$1,766.40
Pebbles Inn	12	1/31/20X3	22	37	16	19	14	17	30	3	158	$379.20
Scotty's Taverns	8	1/31/20X3	74	122	53	63	47	58	101	10	528	$1,267.20
Smokey's Barbeque Pit	8	1/31/20X3	206	339	147	177	132	162	280	29	1472	$3,532.80 *AR.6.1*
Southside Café	8	1/31/20X3	97	160	69	83	62	76	132	13	692	$1,660.80
St. Francis Hotel and Spa	8	1/31/20X3	218	359	156	187	140	172	297	31	1560	$3,744.00

Client Supporting Document

AR.6.7: pg. 1 of 2

Alpine Cupcakes, Inc.
Sales Journal
January 20X3

Name	Deliveries per Month	Sales Date	Carrot Cake	Chocolate	Gluten-free Chocolate	Lemon	Red Velvet	Spice	Vanilla	Vegan	Total Order	Invoice Total
Steinberg Delis	8	1/31/20X3	61	101	44	52	39	48	83	8	436	$1,046.40
The Breakfast Place	12	1/31/20X3	170	279	121	146	109	133	231	24	1213	$2,911.20
The Sandwich Place	8	1/31/20X3	15	25	10	13	9	11	20	2	105	$252.00
UC Boulder Food Service	20	1/31/20X3	652	1071	465	558	419	512	885	93	4655	$11,172.00
UC Denver Food Service	20	1/31/20X3	462	759	330	396	297	363	627	66	3300	$7,920.00
Total Corporate Sales												**$100,528.80**

AR.6.7: pg. 2 of 2

Garcia and Foster, CPAs, LLC

Performed by: *TES*   **Reviewed by:** SDM
Date: *02/14/20X3*   **Date:** 2/15/20x3

We reviewed the Accounts Receivable Aging worksheet and financial statements to determine the process used to identify any allowance for uncollectible accounts. The client has not estimated any allowances for uncollectible accounts in 20X1 or 20X2.

Per discussion with Lisa Mercer, Alpine uses a direct write-off approach for uncollectible accounts receivable balances as necessary. Lisa stated that Alpine Cupcakes has not needed to write off any customer accounts in over 2 years. She credits her careful vetting of corporate sales clients for this success rate. Lisa has determined that the company does not need to book an allowance for uncollectible accounts for 20X2 as all AR balances are deemed to be realizable.

Per our review of the AR aging schedule, AR confirmations and the other AR testing procedures, we have determined that there are no material misstatements with the allowance for uncollectible accounts.